Philip Pullman's Jesus

Philip Pullman's Jesus

Gerald O'Collins

Paulist Press
New York / Mahwah, NJ

First published in 2010 by
Darton, Longman and Todd Ltd
1 Spencer Court
140–142 Wandsworth High Street
London SW18 4JJ

Copyright © 2010 by Gerald O'Collins, SJ

All rights reserved. No part of this book may be reproduced or transmitted in any form or by any means, electronic or mechanical, including photocopying, recording or by any information storage and retrieval system without permission in writing from the publisher.

Library of Congress Control Number: 2011929544

ISBN 978-0-8091-4730-4

North American edition published in 2011 by

Paulist Press, Inc.
997 Macarthur Boulevard
Mahwah, New Jersey 07430
United States of America
www.paulistpress.com

Printed and bound in the United States of America

Contents

Introduction		vii
Chapter One	Jesus Fiction	1
Chapter Two	The Birth of Twins	11
Chapter Three	'Jesus' and 'Christ'	23
Chapter Four	The Teaching of Jesus	33
Chapter Five	The Miracles of Jesus	45
Chapter Six	Only One Source for the Gospels?	55
Chapter Seven	Tampering with the Story	65
Chapter Eight	The Agony in the Garden	75
Chapter Nine	The Death and 'Resurrection' of Jesus	83
Epilogue		93

Pullman's *The Good Man Jesus and the*
   Scoundrel Christ: Interviews and Reviews   101

Index of Names   103

Introduction

Every year or so a book about Jesus appears that makes a great splash. Some of these works, like Hugh Schonfield's *The Passover Plot* (1966), hardly leave a ripple. Other Jesus books, like Albert Schweitzer's *The Quest of the Historical Jesus* (German original, 1906), establish themselves as enduring classics. Some of them, like Dan Brown's *The Da Vinci Code* (2003), teem with historical misinformation, are very badly written, and yet manage to become a gripping read for millions. They prove real page-turners through being a religious exposé, a romance novel and even a murder mystery all in one.[1] Other works on Jesus,

---

1 See my review of *The Da Vinci Code*, the *Pastoral Review* 1 (September-October, 2005), pp. 71–74.

like Gerd Theissen's *The Shadow of the Galilean* (German original, 1986), succeed in wedding the best historical research with an attractive style and real suspense.

In his letter to the Philippians, St Paul remarked about some Christian preachers who neither liked him nor agreed with him: 'others proclaim Christ out of selfish ambition ... What does it matter? Just this, that Christ is proclaimed in every way, whether out of false motives or true; and in that I rejoice' (Philippians 1:17–18).

We might adapt and apply Paul's sentiments. What does it matter why authors like Schonfield, Schweitzer, Brown and Theissen produce books and what they write in them, provided they draw attention to Jesus himself? In that, Christians can rejoice. What, then, of the latest in the crop of Jesus books?

The Talk of the Town

To much fanfare, and on time for last Easter and the Christian celebration of the resurrection, Philip Pullman published *The Good Man Jesus and the Scoundrel Christ*. The reviews have been mixed. In the *Literary Review*, Diarmaid MacCulloch of Oxford University signalled 'the wit and invention of a great storyteller'. But, like Nietzsche, Pullman seems 'obsessed with recovering the "real" Jesus, the affirmer of life, behind the pale abstractions of Christian faith and culture'. 'Much better written' than Jeffrey Archer's *The Gospel According to Judas* but 'certainly offensive', commented Christopher Howse of the London *Daily Telegraph*.

'The Pullman version of the Gospel stories' is 'unchristian' but not 'anti-Jesus', Sally Vickers wrote in the *Daily Telegraph*. Pullman proves a 'supreme story-teller' who reminds readers of the 'extraordinary power' of the Jesus story 'to provoke and disturb'. Yet he gives 'voice to ideologies', not least his visceral antipathy to institutional religion. In the *Guardian*, Rowan Williams, the Archbishop of Canterbury, found Pullman 'deliberately outrageous' and at points ready to indulge 'easy point-scoring'. Nevertheless, he conveys a 'Jesus who was too radical for ordinary human consumption'.

Before presenting and evaluating this latest 'Jesus book', let me describe some of its general features. Pullman's work runs to 245 pages, but over fifty of these pages are completely, or partially, blank. The total word count is low: at the very most, 35,000 words. The shortest of the fifty-three chapters has only one page (the death of John the Baptist), and the longest ('Jesus in the Garden at Gethsemane') runs to just over ten pages.

The large typeface and the 'rubrical' red, chosen for the chapter titles, the running heads and the end papers, give the book a pleasing, even religious look. So too does its white cover embossed with gold, as well as the white ribbon marker of the kind found in old prayer books.

For the most part, the book is beautifully written – as one would expect from a world class master of fantasy fiction. The story moves at a fast pace. The brief chapters encourage readers to keep turning the pages – not least in search of the identity of a central, fictional character. Who is the mysterious and malevolent 'stranger'? Unlike Dan Brown in *The Da Vinci Code*, who eventually reveals the identity of his mysterious 'teacher', Pullman never clearly answers this question.

On the spine of the book, three words stand out: 'Pullman', 'Jesus' and 'Christ' – in that order. On the back cover, a message comes in four words picked out in gold capitals, which many readers may find patronising: 'This is a STORY.'

Pullman and his publishers exploit the ambiguity of a key word. 'Story' may be synonymous with 'history' and could enter the title of a straight historical study: 'The Story of Abraham Lincoln'. 'Story' may also be pure fiction, as when a teacher says to a deceitful child: 'You're telling me a story.'

So what is Pullman's 'story'? A retelling of the history of Jesus? Or a re-writing of that history that begins and ends in fantasy, a radical misrepresentation of the greatest story ever told?

The inside flap assures readers: 'In this ingenious and spellbinding retelling of the life of Jesus, Philip Pullman revisits the most influential story ever told. Charged with mystery, compassion and enormous power, *The Good Man Jesus and the Scoundrel Christ* throws fresh light on who Jesus was.' But does Pullman do more than merely 'revisit' this story? Does he deliberately change and falsify it?

Does Pullman succeed in throwing fresh light 'on who Jesus was'? Or, to use a contrast that recurs repeatedly in his book, does he distort the 'history' of Jesus, in the interest of some alleged, higher 'truth'? No fresh light, but personal ideology? Light not on who Jesus was but on who Pullman is and what he believes?

Over the course of the last two centuries, Jesus books have repeatedly revealed much about their authors. I think of such elegantly written works as D. H. Lawrence's *The Man Who Died* (1931) and Robert Graves' *Jesus in Rome* (1957), as well of such badly written pieces of nonsense as *Holy Blood, Holy Grail* by Michael Baigent, Richard Leigh and Henry Lincoln (1982) and *Jesus the Man* by Barbara Thiering (1992). All four books threw much more light on who their authors were than on Jesus himself.

In Lawrence's novella, Jesus was taken down alive from the cross, revived in the tomb, and walked out, and was cared for by some peasants. When fully recovered, he left for the temple of Isis in Lebanon where he was befriended by the owner of the temple, who believed he was Osiris. He learned with her what 'love' really was, since he had previously denied himself sex. When she became pregnant, he abandoned her with the words: 'So let the boat carry me. Tomorrow is another day.' A reviewer in the *Times Literary Supplement* (2 April 1931) commented: 'So far as Lawrence's attitude to it [reality] is concerned, he seems to have come to the brink and turned away. He has not evaded himself, but he evades Jesus.'

Graves published his reconstruction of how Jesus survived crucifixion and then visited Rome as an allegedly factual, historical account. Graves and his co-author, Joshua Podro, generously supplied information about the 'extreme sultriness of the weather', which, together with the spikenard smeared on the shroud, helped to keep Jesus alive in the tomb. He escaped from the tomb when the Roman soldiers on guard 'rolled back the stone at night while their sergeant was asleep and tried to steal the ointment – which was worth several years' army pay and could easily be sold in the brothels of Caesarea'. They found Jesus alive and let him go. Surprisingly, Graves and Podro did not indulge a taste for *cherchez la femme* and arrange for Jesus to have a rendezvous with a priestess of Isis (as did Lawrence) or with Mary Magdalene (as others have).

Holy Blood, Holy Grail claimed that Jesus was the bridegroom of the marriage feast of Cana, the bride being Mary Magdalene. They subsequently had a number of children, including Barabbas! Jesus was put on a cross by Pilate but taken down alive and never rose from the dead. Mary Magdalene escaped with the children to France. There, the Jesus bloodline was supposed to have continued through the Merovingians, the Carolingians and the House of Lorraine, right down to the Hapsburgs and other noble, royal or imperial families of today. Baigent, Leigh and Lincoln were confident that they had not 'compromised or belittled Jesus'. Their 'investigations' served to replace the 'incomplete' figure of 'established Christianity' with a 'living and plausible Jesus – a Jesus whose life is both meaningful and comprehensible to modern man'.

In the book that made her famous (or merely notorious?), Thiering used her own private 'method' for decoding the Dead Sea Scrolls, a method that serious scholars of various religious faiths or none found utterly implausible. She argued that Jesus was crucified at Qumran (near the Dead Sea), taken down alive, resumed his married life with Mary Magdalene, divorced her to marry Lydia (of Acts 16), and passed his old age in Rome. Thiering 'explained' that Lydia's dealing in 'purple cloth' meant that she sold bishoprics at a price! The 'Lord opening her heart' was understood to be Jesus having relations with her! Thiering expressed the hope that by decoding the New Testament and giving us Jesus' 'true' story, she would help readers strip away the mystery and see him as 'a real, human, fallible figure'. 'Fallible'

Introduction

presumably referred to the breakdown of his first marriage, the divorce, and subsequent union with Lydia.

What they wrote about Jesus tells readers a great deal about Lawrence, Graves, the trio of Baigent, Leigh and Lincoln, and Thiering. Does this latest work reveal more about Pullman and his mindset and less about the historical Jesus? Has Pullman looked down the well of history and seen his own face reflected at the bottom?

With affectionate thanks, I dedicate this book to those who live and work at 9 and 11 Edge Hill, Wimbledon. When I was stranded in England by last April's volcanic ash cloud, they gave me a home and an office in which I wrote the first chapters of this book. I also wish to thank Dan Kendall SJ and others at the University of San Francisco for their hospitality en route back to Australia; and giving me further opportunities for working on this book.

Gerald O'Collins SJ, 16 June 2010
Jesuit Theological College,
Parkville, 3052, Australia

Chapter One

Jesus Fiction

Philip Pullman shows no doubts about the historical existence of Jesus of Nazareth and about much of his teaching and other activity. What constraints does that involve when he or other writers set themselves to flesh out the record imaginatively and bring it alive? Is their autonomy as writers of historical fiction in any way constrained?

Historical Fiction

Those who write novels about totally fictional characters who live in an imaginary place and at an imaginary time enjoy complete freedom in creating events, dialogue, scenery and the rest. J. R. R. Tolkien had such freedom when developing his fantasy adventures *The Hobbit* (1937) and *The Lord of the Rings* (1954–55). He set these adventures in Middle Earth, an imaginary land occupied by hobbits and further mythical creatures.

But those novelists who write about Jesus and other persons who belonged to human history and left well-documented lives write under the constraints of the available evidence. To be sure, they can and should invent dialogue and, where advisable, create and add further characters to the cast of their novels, as well as attending to psychological interactions, scenery and weather. But readers expect authors of historical fiction to remain faithful to the known, central facts. They will not be amused to find the assassination of Julius Caesar shifted from Rome to Alexandria. Nor would they look with favour on an author who took the liberty of inventing a secret marriage between Queen Elizabeth I and Philip II of Spain. Writers of historical fiction may not play fast and loose with history.

Here, George MacDonald Fraser (1925–2008) deserves an honourable mention. For his *Flashman* novels, he invented Harry Paget Flashman, a notorious cad and womaniser. But the nineteenth-century wars and adventures that this picaresque antihero survived are described by Fraser with careful accuracy about the known historical details. These novels provide a charming and impeccable introduction to many episodes in British and American history. Where else would you learn that the Charge of the Light Brigade and the Charge of the Heavy Brigade took place on the same day in 1854 at the Battle of Balaclava during the Crimean War? Naturally, Flashman took part in both charges and emerged alive at the end of a long and dangerous day.

Jesus Fiction

Fictional works about Jesus continue to flourish in modern times. Dorothy Sayers set a high standard with her *Man Born to be King*, a radio version of the Jesus story that the BBC broadcast (December 1941–October 1942). In the published version she explains how she drew on such scholars as Archbishop William Temple and Sir Edwyn Hoskyns, how she interpreted the major characters in her Jesus story, what principles she used when developing dialogue (for instance, between King Herod and the wise men), and what she aimed at when inventing additional characters.

In a different medium, the novelist Anthony Burgess matched Sayers when he co-wrote the film script for Franco Zeffirelli's extraordinary television miniseries, *Jesus of Nazareth* (1977). Burgess deftly added dialogue and further characters, while preserving the main outlines of the Gospel story.

Another highly successful fictional account of Jesus came from Gerd Theissen. For *The Shadow of the Galilean* (English translation, 1987), he created Andreas, son of John from Sepphoris, a large and flourishing city some miles from Nazareth. In the service of Pontius Pilate, Andreas goes in search of Jesus and reports very accurately all the information he gains about Jesus from particular individuals and various groups, like the Pharisees and Sadducees. Everywhere, Andreas discovers the impact that Jesus has been making on crowds and individuals. But he never succeeds in personally meeting Jesus. The novel ends with Andreas on the walls of Jerusalem, looking out at Jesus dead on a cross.

Other writers have exploited a similar technique. They create characters who tell the story of

Jesus through what they have experienced of him or at least learned about him.

In yet further cases the writers themselves are the narrators. That is what Pullman does; he tells the story of Jesus in his own name and massively refashions it in a flat, laconic style. He deliberately refrains from adding description, landscape, and (for the most part) psychological detail.

A notable newcomer to Jesus fiction is Anne Rice, born in 1946, just five years before Pullman. Her chronicles of vampires and witches, not to mention several erotic novels, sold nearly one million copies before she returned to the faith of her childhood. She then decided to dedicate her mature years to writing a multi-volume account of Jesus, entitled *Christ the Lord*. After *Out of Egypt* (2005) she published *The Road to Cana* (2008). A third volume, *The Kingdom of Heaven*, is still to come.

Rice has become a friend of an outstanding New Testament scholar, Craig Keener, who in 2009 published a landmark volume, *The Historical Jesus of the Gospels*. In writing her Jesus novels, Rice draws on Keener for his examination of the Gospel accounts and historical conclusions. She shows a novelist's flair by filling in blanks in the record of Jesus' life provided by the Gospels, thinking up details for the setting of episodes, and developing personalities and dialogue. Thus, *The Road to Cana* imaginatively re-creates much of the story for the years Jesus spent in Nazareth before being baptised by John.

Jesus himself remains centrally present in Rice's narrative. In fact, in *The Road to Cana* he is the narrator. She boldly lets him tell his own story.

The work of Fraser, Sayers, Burgess, Theissen and Rice raises some questions for Pullman, who with *The Good Man Jesus and the Scoundrel Christ* has moved from what he has done so well, fantasy fiction, to a new field, historical fiction. Did he exempt himself from doing any background historical research into current scholarship on the Gospels and the life of Jesus?

In an interview with Laura Barton (the *Guardian*, 19 April 2010), Pullman mentioned four authors that he read before writing *The Good Man Jesus and the Scoundrel Christ*: the Oxford scholar Geza Vermes, Pope Benedict XVI, A. N. Wilson, and David Friedrich Strauss. None of these four writers represent the best of current scholarship on the historical Jesus. Pullman chose a curious foursome to prepare himself for his venture into Jesus fiction.

A valuable contributor to studies of the Dead Sea Scrolls, Vermes, thirty-seven years ago with his *Jesus the Jew* (1973), encouraged others to take seriously the Jewishness of Jesus. But Pullman's evaluation of Vermes as '*the foremost* Jesus scholar' (italics mine) would not be accepted by the New Testament experts of today. Pope Benedict's *Jesus of Nazareth* (2007) expresses movingly the way in which the life of Jesus has nourished the faith of the present Pope, an outstanding theologian but no biblical scholar.

Wilson, an eloquent writer but again no biblical scholar, has distanced himself from his 1992 book *Jesus* and its misguided attempt to undermine the resurrection of Jesus. In a review of Pullman's *The Good Man Jesus and the Scoundrel Christ*, Wilson vigorously attacks its version of the Jesus story and, in particular, its rejection of a true resurrection (the *Spectator*, 3 April 2010). In his famous (or notorious?) 1835 *Life of Jesus*, Strauss questioned all the supernatural elements in the Gospel stories, which he described as 'myth' or creative legends developed after the death of Jesus. He 'explained' the growth of early Christianity philosophically, in terms of a Hegelian dialectic. It is hard to imagine how the books by Vermes, Benedict XVI, Wilson and Strauss could have prepared Pullman adequately for his step into Jesus fiction.

In his interview with Barton, Pullman excused himself from reading further 'commentators' on the grounds that they might have inhibited imagination. That meant no contact with such contemporary New Testament specialists in the history of Jesus as Dale Allison, Richard Bauckham, James Dunn, Martin Hengel, Craig Keener, John Meier and Tom Wright.

Some knowledge of the commentators might have saved Pullman from various historical errors, like: (1) He alleges that John 'invented the rite of baptism' (p. 32). Washing ceremonies to cleanse from sins and impurity already existed in Judaism, notably among the Essenes on the Dead Sea; (2) Many scholars now doubt what Pullman suggests about the Zealots, that groups of them were active at the time of Jesus' death (p. 68). Earlier or later Zealots engaged in terrorist actions, yes, but not right at the time when Jesus died; (3) Contact with the scholars could have made Pullman think twice about fabricating only one source of all four Gospels: the work of Jesus' twin brother. That strange notion deserves chapter-length treatment (see Chapter 6 below).

If Pullman failed to take advantage of the true experts, did he also decline to be constrained even by the text of the Gospels themselves? Did he feel free to alter the story over and over again in the interests of his own 'truth' or ideology? That seems to be the case.

On page one, Pullman introduces Mary of Nazareth, who – 'as the world knows' – was the mother of Jesus. At once he adds something 'the world does not know': that Jesus had a twin brother, given 'a common name' (that is never specified) but called 'Christ' (p. 21).

Right from the outset, Pullman asserts his freedom not only to cite history ('what the world knows') but also to rewrite history in the interests of his own 'story'.

Chapter Two

The Birth of Twins

Pullman begins 'the story of Jesus and his brother Christ' by telling how their mother Mary was born to 'a rich, pious and elderly couple', Joachim and Anna, and then left in the care of 'the high priest Zacharias', whose wife was named Elizabeth. He raised the little girl 'like a dove' and 'everyone loved her for her grace and simplicity'.

When Mary was twelve years old, an angel told Zacharias what he should do: find an older and steady husband for her, preferably a widower. So Zacharias called together a dozen or more widowers, who were all to bring a rod with them. One of the widowers was a carpenter named Joseph. Zacharias prayed over the rods and gave them back to the widowers. When Joseph received his rod, it 'burst into flower'. That was the sign that he should take Mary in marriage and bring her home to his house.

But then Joseph went away on work for a long time, apparently for four years. During this strange absence, Mary grew to be a young woman and caught the interest of the young men hanging around the streets of Nazareth.

One night she heard a whisper through her bedroom window. An 'angel', with the appearance of a young man, said that he wanted to tell her a secret that only she should know. So Mary let the 'angel' into her bedroom and was told that the Lord wanted her to conceive at once a child. The 'angel' had come to bring this about. With a hint and wink, the story implies that one of the local boys seduced Mary.

When Joseph returned from his long absence, he found Mary with child. Unlike in Matthew 1:20–21, no angel appeared to Joseph to assure him that the child had been conceived through the power of the Holy Spirit. Yet, on his own initiative, Joseph decided to look after Mary.

When the Roman emperor decreed that everyone should return to their ancestral home to be counted in a census, Joseph took Mary to Bethlehem. He made Mary comfortable in a stable and then ran to find a midwife. When he returned, a child was already born. But the midwife said: 'There's another to come. She's having twins.' Sure enough, Mary gave birth to twins: first, the one who was to be called 'Jesus' and, then, his sickly brother who was to be called 'Christ'.

That very night, an angel directed some shepherds, 'pious Jews', to find the newborn 'Messiah' lying in an animal's feeding trough. The shepherds paid their homage to Christ, as Mary had set him down in the trough while she nursed her other child, Jesus.

Soon after that some astrologers turned up from the East with their gifts. No gleaming star led them on their search for the King of the Jews, but rather the observations they had made of the planets. Their visit prompted King Herod to order the slaughter of 'every child' in Bethlehem and the neighbourhood under two years of age.

One of the children of 'the right age' was John, a son born to older parents, Zacharias and Elizabeth. They managed to hide him in a cave. But Herod sent for Zacharias, who refused to say where his son was to be found. So Herod spilled the blood of the old priest, who died a martyr's death.

Did Pullman confuse the father of John the Baptist with Zacharias the son of Barachiah, 'murdered between the sanctuary and the altar' (Matthew 23:35; see Luke 11:51)? This Zacharias was an ancient prophet assassinated by King Joash and his officials (2 Chronicles 24:20–22).

Whatever the source for Pullman giving the father of the Baptist a martyr's death, at all events he has Joseph managing to escape with Mary and the twins to Egypt.

Pullman's 'Adaptation' of Matthew and Luke

Before pressing on with Pullman's book, we might pause to spell out the sources from which he has so far spun his tale. From Matthew he has drawn the visit of the astrologers, the flight into Egypt and the slaughter of the innocents. Luke provides the names of Zacharias and Elizabeth, the story of the birth of their son, and the Roman census that brought Mary and Joseph to Bethlehem.

Pullman rewrites some of what he has found in Matthew and Luke. Unlike Pullman, Matthew tells of Mary being found with child *before* she went to live in the house of Joseph, not while she was living there while he was absent for four years.

Matthew and Luke would have been astonished to find the shepherds described as 'pious Jews'; their way of life made it impossible for them to follow the Jewish law properly.

While Matthew writes of the slaughter of the innocents, he specifies that Herod ordered the death of every *male* child of two years or under (Matthew 2:26), not every child irrespective of their sex. Moreover, Matthew has nothing to say about the killing of the father of John the Baptist. In any case, Zacharias and Elizabeth are said to have lived in 'the hill country of Judea' (Luke 1:39) and not where the killing of the innocents is supposed to have taken place: in Bethlehem or its neighbourhood.

Pullman tampers with the material he takes from Luke. The evangelist knows nothing of Zacharias being the high priest, let alone being a high priest under whose care Mary spent the first twelve years of her life. His rank is much lower; he belonged to a section of the priesthood called Abijah (Luke 1:5). It is hard to see how much Pullman gains by promoting Zacharias to being the high priest who raised Mary and by making him a martyr, the only adult martyred by Herod along with the holy innocents. Perhaps giving Zacharias a role in the life of Mary and in the massacre of the innocents builds up a character whose role in Luke's Gospel is limited to the conception and birth of John the Baptist. This allows Zacharias to be something of a noble counterpart to the villainous Herod the Great.

Pullman selects some features and words from Luke's account of the Annunciation but leaves that account behind by turning it into an episode that took place *at night in Mary's bedroom.* Luke specifies neither the place nor the time of day or night for the Annunciation. Much more seriously, according to Luke (and Matthew) Mary conceives her son through the power of the Holy Spirit. Pullman leaves his readers with the strong suggestion that it was a young man masquerading as an angel who persuaded Mary to open the door and let him in. So much for the virginal conception!

Pullman's Other Sources

As well as picking, choosing and changing what he wants from the first-century Gospels of Matthew and Luke, Pullman has taken various details from much later sources. That the parents of Mary were called Joachim and Anna is a later tradition, not found in the New Testament. That

Mary was presented in the Temple in Jerusalem and grew up there is the stuff of later legends and paintings, even if both Western and Eastern Christians celebrate the Presentation of the Blessed Virgin Mary on 21 November.

Such works as the *Book of James*, also called the *Protoevangelium* (second century), and the *History of Joseph the Carpenter* (fourth to seventh century) speak of Jesus being an elderly widower at the time of his marriage to Mary and about him hunting for a midwife when she gave birth in Bethlehem. They provide some charming stories about Joseph, including the detail about the rod of Joseph bursting into flower.

In an article in the *Daily Telegraph* (7 April 2010), Pullman mentions M. R. James' 1924 translation, *The Apocryphal New Testament*. But I wonder how much he studied this work. Does he simply weave in items about Joachim, Anna, Mary and Joseph that he heard long ago in Sunday School?

What's in their Names?

To the surprise and bewilderment of many readers, Pullman divides the historical figure known as

Jesus Christ into fictional twins, Jesus and Christ. Before asking why Pullman does this, let me insert some background information.

Recent archaeological discoveries have created a data bank of the names given to men and women in first-century Palestine. Sacred and secular texts had already provided much information. Various names turn up, for instance, in the works of the Jewish historian Josephus. The books of the New Testament also record many names used at the time of Jesus. But now excavations of ancient tombs and the publication of the Dead Sea Scrolls have added an impressive amount of further information about names which parents gave their children at that time.

'Mary' and 'Salome' headed the list of personal names given to daughters. 'Simon' or 'Simeon' and 'Joseph' or 'Joses' were the most popular names chosen for sons. Many of the favourite names are familiar to us from the New Testament: 'Martha', 'Lazarus' or 'Eleazar', and 'Jesus' or 'Joshua'. Inscriptions on tombs have added many more examples of such names. In the case of 'Jesus', we find that personal name around one hundred times. This includes the case of a disciple called 'Jesus', who had the nickname of 'the just one' (Colossians 4:11).

The Birth of Twins

What may be surprising is that three famous personal names are conspicuously absent from inscriptions on tombs and the ancient texts: 'Moses', 'David' and 'Elijah'. Many Jews at that time expected the coming of a prophet, priest and leader like Moses, which had been promised by Deuteronomy 18:18–19. Many too hoped for a royal Messiah, who would be descended from David. The prophet Elijah, who also on occasions acted like a priest, had been taken up into heaven in a fiery chariot (2 Kings 2:1–13). People looked for his return.

So far, no tomb or text has revealed the existence of any contemporary of Jesus who was called Moses or David or Elijah. We do not have to look far for a reason why these great names were passed over. Jewish parents in first-century Palestine who chose for their son one of these three names would have been announcing to the world: 'Our boy is in fact Elijah come back to earth. Our boy is the long-expected royal king from the house of David. Our boy will be the new Moses to deliver us from oppression.' At the time of Jesus, it would have been a remarkable and even dangerous act of presumption on the part of Jewish parents to have chosen Moses or David or Elijah as the personal name for their male child.

Still less could or would they have called their son 'Christ'. It means, as Pullman knows, 'the Anointed One' or 'Messiah'. The word functioned as a *title* for the kingly or priestly liberator/leader expected by many Jews at the time. During the lifetime of Jesus, some of his followers already applied this title to him. Most famously, Simon Peter answered Jesus' question 'Who do you say that I am?' by saying: 'You are the Christ' (Mark 8:27–29).

After the death and resurrection of Jesus, his followers quickly gave him the title of 'Christ' or 'Messiah'. They confessed their faith in him by announcing: 'Jesus is the Christ. Jesus is the Messiah we have been expecting; God has finally sent him.'

Before long, the personal name and the title were run together. Disciples spoke of 'Jesus Christ'. The way was open for the name and the title to become a first and second name, and function in the way they do today when we speak of Michael Smith, Danielle Mann or Alan Wong. The way was also quickly open for disciples to refer to Jesus by what had become his second name. This is what an early piece of proclamation quoted by Paul does. He writes to the Corinthians: 'I handed on to you what I also received: that

Christ died for our sins according to the Scriptures' (1 Corinthians 15:3).

But, as we saw above, in first-century Palestine 'Christ' or 'Messiah' was *never* a personal name. It was the title given to the royal and/or priestly agent who was expected to be sent by God. Pullman evidently knows that. What personal agenda persuaded him to promote an impossible idea and give the personal name of 'Christ' to an alleged twin brother of Jesus? And, in any case, where did Pullman find the notion of Mary giving birth to twins?

In a telephone interview with Vit Wagner (*Toronto Star*, 10 April 2010), Pullman stated that he did not mean to suggest that the historical Jesus had a twin brother: 'It's a fable', a story, 'to illustrate a point. I'm telling a story about Jesus and I give him a twin brother to illustrate my belief that the man and the myth are something different.' The man Jesus 'was true. But the god was made up.'

This answer raises several questions. May a writer mix history and fable in this way? (We come back to this issue in the epilogue.) Are 'fable' and 'myth' interchangeable or even synonymous, as Pullman implies? Entries on 'fable' and 'myth' in the *Oxford English Dictionary* suggest otherwise.

In any case, is 'myth' always something 'made up' and untrue? With reference to his book, Pullman apparently wants to say just that. The (historical) man is 'true', but Jesus' divinity ('the god') is only 'made up' and untrue. We come back later to this issue.

In the next chapter, we look further at the way Pullman himself has 'made up' a twin for Jesus and why he has done so. His aim is obviously to cast doubt on the 'myth', or belief in the divine identity of Jesus.

Chapter Three

'Jesus' and 'Christ'

To begin with, I thought that Pullman's fictional theory of twins might have been prompted by his reading of John's Gospel, where the apostle Thomas is three times called by the nickname of 'Didymus' or 'the Twin' (John 11:16; 20:24; 21:2). Most likely this was a nickname used by early Christians, a way of distinguishing him from numerous other men who were also called 'Thomas'. John's Gospel never identifies the twin brother or sister of Thomas.

It was left to an apocryphal work written in the third century, the *Acts of Thomas*, to suggest that Thomas the apostle was the twin brother of Jesus. What better way to heighten the fame of Thomas!

The *Acts of Thomas* betrays its Gnostic origins by repeatedly depreciating marriage. Ancient and modern Gnostics imagine that special knowledge will bring redemption, and that redemption involves the human spirit escaping the evil condition of matter and reaching a spiritual world of light. Such a mindset cannot appreciate the dignity of the human body and the holiness of married life. It can make nothing of a future destiny that brings the resurrection and transformation of the body.

In an interview with Laura Barton (the *Guardian*, 19 April 2010), Pullman recalled that he went through 'a very Gnostic phase' in his twenties but gradually abandoned his engagement with Gnosticism. Perhaps a vague memory of a twin assigned to Jesus in the Gnostic-tinged *Acts of Thomas* fed into Pullman's choice. He himself explained matters differently.

A Revealing Interview

In an interview with Brian Appleyard (the *Sunday Times*, 28 March 2010), Pullman associated his choice with his re-reading of the letters of St Paul: 'I counted 30 occasions when he [Paul] refers to

Jesus but 150-plus when he refers to Christ. Paul wasn't interested in Jesus, he was interested in Christ – in the God part, not the man part.' Paul, he added, 'was an incomparable genius, literary and administrative, whose view of this entity he called Jesus Christ, strongly skewed towards the Christ part, is what the Church has been founded on ever since.'

There is much to challenge here. (1) Paul was surely a spiritual, mystical genius or a heroic saint and martyr, and not primarily a literary and administrative genius. In any case, describing him an 'administrative genius' seems a bit odd, in the light of the troubles he had with communities he had himself founded in Corinth and elsewhere. (2) He called Jesus Christ not an 'entity' but the person to whom, after their meeting on the Damascus Road, he passionately devoted his whole life (Galatians 2:20; Philippians 3:8–11). (3) If Pullman had taken the trouble of checking any standard concordance of the seven letters that certainly come directly from Paul (Romans, 1 and 2 Corinthians, Galatians, Philippians, 1 Thessalonians and Philemon), he could have corrected his statistics and found that the apostle refers to 'Jesus' 144 times and 'Christ' 269 times. Certainly, Paul prefers 'Christ' over 'Jesus'. But it is not even a two-to-one preference, let alone the more than five-to-one preference alleged by Pullman.

(4) Moreover, did Paul fail to show interest in the earthly, historical Jesus, 'the man part'? This claim does not stand scrutiny. Paul tells us that Jesus was a Jew (Galatians 4:4), born of the house of David (Romans 1:3). He quotes some of his teaching (1 Corinthians 7:10–11), is the first New Testament writer to give us an account of Jesus celebrating the Last Supper on the night before he was handed over (1 Corinthians 11:23–27), and returns over and over again to the horrendous death of Jesus on the cross (e.g. 1 Corinthians 1:13, 23; Galatians 3:1, 13). When Paul lists those to whom the risen Lord appeared (1 Corinthians 15:5–8), they met, as the context shows, the same Jesus who had lived on earth, called the Twelve and, in particular, Peter, and ended by being executed and buried (1 Corinthians 15:3–5). They knew the risen Lord to be identical with the Jesus of history, Pullman's 'man-part'.

Recent New Testament scholarship, led by Richard Hays, Morna Hooker, J. L. Martyn, and Thomas Stegman, has made it even harder for those who allege that Paul showed little interest in the earthly Jesus. It has re-opened the question of a phrase that recurs seven times in the apostle's certainly authentic letters: 'the faith of Jesus Christ' (e.g. Romans 3:22) or 'the faith of Jesus' (e.g. Romans 3:26). Instead of interpreting this expression as speaking of *our faith in Jesus Christ* (an 'objective' genitive), these scholars now understand it to refer primarily to the *faithful obedience exercised by the historical Jesus* in his life and death (a 'subjective' genitive). That means that the commitment of faith practised by Jesus was supremely important for Paul – in fact, the lynchpin in his understanding the justification of sinful human beings.

Thus, contemporary scholarship has made it even more difficult for those like Pullman who credit Paul with little interest in the historical Jesus.

(5) I puzzled too over Pullman associating 'the God part' with the title 'Christ'. The seven clearly authentic letters of Paul show the apostle expressing 'the God part' not through the title of 'Christ' but through other titles: 'Son of God' (thirteen times) and, above all, 'Lord' (at least 170 times). The risen and exalted Jesus receives the divine title of 'Lord' and the adoration of the universe that belongs only to God (Philippians 2:9–11).

In the hymn he quotes (or perhaps composes) in Philippians 2, Paul confesses his faith in Jesus as divine Lord. Larry Hurtado and other contemporary scholars have shown how, in making that confession, the apostle professes the common faith of early Christians.

(6) Finally, in his interview Pullman blames the apostle Paul for 'skewing' institutional Christianity towards the 'the God part', or towards a lopsided emphasis on the divinity of Jesus. But, as we shall see, the revelation of Jesus as the Son of God was rooted in his life and ministry. Belief in his divinity was not something introduced and first propagated by Paul. It was already held by Christians before Paul became one himself.

What Pullman said in his interview with Appleyard could shift our attention from the real villain of his story, 'the scoundrel Christ' who is the twin brother of Jesus. He is the one who, prompted by a mysterious 'stranger', 'skewed' – that is to say, deliberately falsified – the record. He is the one who misrepresented the pure moral voice of his brother and manipulated history in order to found a loathsome institution, the Church. To bring that about, Christ betrays his brother to execution and then impersonates him in the guise of Jesus risen from the dead. But more of all that later.

Another Revealing Interview

In an interview with Erica Wagner (*The Times*, 3 April 2010), when explaining his creation of the twins, Pullman cited Paul again but this time also referred to the Gospels: 'For the Gospel writers, whoever they were, Jesus the man was in some ways the more important thing. Some of them don't even refer to him, particularly, as God.' Pullman used here slightly more careful language. If, for the Gospel writers, 'Jesus the man was in some ways the more important thing', this implies that for them Jesus the God did not lack importance.

In fact, all four Gospel writers present the divinity of Jesus. The first Gospel to be written, that by Mark, begins with the identity of Jesus as divine Son of God (Mark 1:1, 11). At the halfway mark, in the episode of the Transfiguration, the voice of the Father recognises Jesus as his beloved Son (Mark 9:7). The climax of the Gospel comes immediately after the crucifixion, when the centurion in charge of the crucifixion becomes the first human being on earth to recognise the true identity of Jesus: 'Indeed, this man was Son of God' (Mark 15:39).

It would be bizarre to allege that the Gospel of John 'doesn't refer to Jesus, particularly, as God'. It begins with the majestic announcement: 'In the beginning was the Word and the Word was with God, and the Word was God' (John 1:1). That Gospel reaches its final high point with Thomas the Apostle gazing at Jesus and saying: 'My Lord and my God' (John 20:28).

In the interview with Erica Wagner, once again Pullman revealed that he associated 'Jesus' with the human side and 'Christ' with the divine side. This, of course, was to slide over the fact that, as such, the title 'Christ' referred to some anointed human figure, a kingly or priestly liberator sent by God. The personal name 'Jesus' and the title 'Christ' cannot be distinguished by claiming that the former points to humanity and the latter to divinity.

Add to this a further odd feature: in Pullman's story the fictional twins, 'Jesus' and 'Christ', are *not* in fact distinguished by one (Jesus) being human and the other (Christ) being divine. In the story, they are both thoroughly human.

What happens rather is that the second born of the twins, Christ, deliberately falsifies for posterity the history of his brother and so fashions a 'truth' – that is to say the big lie on which organised Christianity would be built: the divinity of Jesus. This 'truth' (read 'lie') gave institutional leaders the unquestioned authority they would want for themselves.

To justify Pullman's association of 'Christ' with 'the God part', one might say that the Christ of his story bears the blame, along with the mysterious 'stranger', for creating and selling to the Church the false notion of his twin brother Jesus being the incarnate Son of God. In *that* sense 'the God part' is linked with the figure of 'Christ' but only in the story that Pullman himself has made up.

Perhaps one should not spend too much time looking for reasons based on biblical and historical records to account for the names Pullman gave his fictional twins. As he said to Wagner, 'Jesus Christ' seemed to him like 'two parts of an atom that want to spring apart'. So he separated them and turned them into twin brothers.

Jung and the Shadow

As an author who reacts with irritated disbelief to any reviewers who 'explain' in psychological terms what I have written, I am reluctant to do the same for *The Good Man Jesus and the Scoundrel Christ*. But a comment from a cherished friend, about

'Christ' representing the shadow side of Jesus, rang a bell for me.

Pullman retells the scene in the Gospels where Satan tempts Jesus in the wilderness by replacing Satan with 'Christ'. The tempter of Jesus becomes 'none other than his own shadow, his twin Christ'. In a *Sunday Telegraph* review (11 April 2010), Rowan Somerville reflected further on the way Pullman has rewritten the temptation in the desert: 'After all, who is it in our own lives who whispers that we should do terrible things: an external demon or our own, self-serving desires?'

My friend, and then Somerville, pushed me in a Jungian direction, at least to account for the way Pullman takes away from Satan his most significant appearance in the Gospel story and assigns it to 'Christ'. But can such a Jungian explanation work for what 'Christ' will go on to do in Pullman's story: the persistent falsification of Jesus' activity, the Judas-style betrayal in Gethsemane, and the masquerading as his brother allegedly risen from the dead? As the book develops, the twins pull apart too much for those who want to find a Jungian story in the text. 'Christ' cannot be read as the shadow side of the individual Jesus.

Chapter Four

The Teaching of Jesus

The teaching of Jesus wins sincere praise from Pullman: 'he's a very attractive figure. He was one of the greatest storytellers of all time (and of course that interests me), and he had an unparalleled gift for making phrases that linger in the memory with the force of revelation' (interview with Jo Case, *Readings Monthly*, May 2010).

The phrase of Jesus about 'whited sepulchres' led Pullman in that interview to speak out once again against organised religion: 'when you consider the poor, wandering, hand-to-mouth figure of this peripatetic prophet and healer, who had no place to lay his head, and you compare him with the fantastic and unimaginable wealth or splendour of the Pope in all his glory and his power, what can you do but ... well, shake your head?'

Packing a Punch

The way Pullman retells the story of what Jesus taught and said, he frequently lets a voice of genuine spiritual authority come through. His version of a familiar saying or narrative often conveys what Archbishop Rowan Williams (the *Guardian*, 3 April 2010) calls 'a pitch-perfect rendering in modern idiom, carrying something of the shock and compelling attraction of the original gospel text'.

The Archbishop gives an example: 'when he [Pullman] relates the story of Jesus healing a demon-possessed man in the synagogue, his Jesus responds to the shouts of the disturbed man with, "You can be quiet now. He's gone away" – subtly paraphrasing the "be silent and come out of him" in the gospel.' Rowan Williams comments: 'This eloquently suggests the sort of sense a modern reader might make of the story, without reducing the manifest authority of the words of Jesus.'

My own favourite example is Pullman's vivid and effective rendering of the exchange with a lawyer that led Jesus to tell the parable of the Good Samaritan (Luke 10:28–37). The lawyer began by asking: 'Teacher, what must I do to inherit eternal life?' Jesus prompted the lawyer into citing what the law says: 'You must love the Lord God with all your heart, and with all your soul, and with all your strength, and with all your mind. And you must love your neighbour as you love yourself.' 'That's it,' said Jesus, 'you've got it. You know the law. Do that, and you'll live.'

Then, in response to the lawyer's question, 'who is my neighbour?', Jesus told the story of the wounded traveller and the Samaritan who helped him.

When asked by Jesus: who proved 'a neighbour to the man who was robbed on the Jericho road'?, the lawyer could only answer: 'The one who helped him'. 'That's all you need to know,' said Jesus. 'Off you go, and do the same thing.' Pullman's rendering of the conclusion packs a punch when set over against the usual version: 'Go and do likewise.'

Sermon on the Mount

Pullman spends two chapters retelling the Sermon on the Mount – in his words, 'Jesus Preaches on a

Mountain'. The first of these two chapters paraphrases the Beatitudes, from Matthew 5:3–12 and Luke 6:20–23, and the woes from Luke 6:24–26 ('there will be some who will be cursed, who will never inherit the Kingdom of God').

Pullman maintains Jesus' language about the Kingdom of God, but tips the message of the Beatitudes away from 'loving the Lord God' in the direction of 'loving your neighbour as you love yourself'. Let me give an example, the sixth of Matthew's Beatitudes. It is usually translated: 'Blessed are the pure of heart. They shall see God.' God disappears in Pullman's rendering of what being 'pure in heart' will bring: 'Those who are pure in heart and think no evil of others – they will be blessed.' This interpretation fails to match the sense commentators normally find in this Beatitude: purity of heart involves fidelity to the divine commands and sincere worship of God.

The three chapters in Matthew's Sermon on the Mount (Matthew 5–7) have entered the imagination of the world. For many, Christians and others alike, these chapters present the most sublime and compelling code of human conduct that they have ever read. I can understand why some reviewers found Pullman's introduction flat, almost as if Jesus were speaking to children in a primary school: 'And today I'm going to tell you who's going to be received into the Kingdom, and who isn't, so pay attention.'

The Absences

What disturbs me about Pullman's presentation of the teaching of Jesus is the significant material that he leaves out. In a chapter entitled 'Difficult Stories' he paraphrases attractively three parables: the Labourers in the Vineyard (Matthew 20:1–16), the Crafty Manager (Luke 16:1–8) and the Pharisee and the Tax Collector (Luke 18:9–14). But Pullman omits what we might call the 'difficult teaching', those passages where Jesus implied that he possessed an authority that put him on a par with God.

Jesus spoke with his own authority, at times prefacing his teaching with 'I say to you' (Matthew 5:21–44) and not with such prophetic rubrics as 'thus says the Lord' or 'oracle of the Lord'. It was above all the 'objects' over which he asserted authority that made such claims startling. Either by what he said or by what he did (or both), Jesus claimed authority over the observance of the Sabbath (e.g. Mark 2:23–28; 3:1–5), the Temple

(Mark 11:15–17), and the Law – three divinely authorised channels of salvation. Let me briefly recall some aspects of the authoritative attitude towards the divine Law and the Temple that Jesus showed in his ministry and that Pullman leaves out of consideration.

Jesus took it upon himself not only to criticise the *oral law* for running counter to basic human obligations (Mark 7:9–13) but also to set aside the *written law* on such matters as retribution, divorce, oaths, and food (Matthew 5:21–48; Mark 7:15, 19). This was to put himself on a par with the divine Lord who had prescribed on these matters through Moses: 'Of old it was said to you by God speaking through Moses, but I say to you.' Apropos of the Temple saying, it is admittedly hard to establish its original form (Mark 14:57–59; Acts 6:13–14). But it involved some claim that his mission was to bring a new relationship between God and the chosen people, which would supplant the central place of the current relationship, the Temple in Jerusalem. Jesus was himself to replace the Temple and its cult with something better ('not made by human hands').

Seemingly on a level with Jesus' astonishing assertion of his personal rights over the day, place, and law of Jewish life, was his willingness to dispense with the divinely established channels for the forgiveness of sins (sacrificial offerings in the Temple and the mediation of priestly authorities) and to take on God's role by forgiving sins in his own name. He did this by word (Mark 2:1–11; Luke 7:47–49) and by table fellowship with sinners. Jesus claimed the authority to mediate the forgiveness of sins committed against God.

Jesus used his favourite self-designation, 'Son of Man', when claiming to be decisive for the final relationship between human beings and God: 'every one who acknowledges me before human beings, the Son of Man will acknowledge before the angels of God. But those who deny me before human beings will be denied before the angels of God' (Luke 12:8–9). Jesus understood the full and final salvation of human beings to depend upon their present relationship with him.

In these and other ways, during his ministry Jesus gave the impression of setting himself on a par with God. One can understand members of the Sanhedrin charging Jesus with blasphemy. They feared that he was not merely a false prophet but was even usurping divine prerogatives (Mark 14:64). In his chapter on the trial of Jesus ('Jesus before the Council'), Pullman carefully skirts around this issue.

Besides avoiding passages where Jesus implicitly claimed for himself divine authority, Pullman deftly modifies some episodes, so as to shift attention away from the person of Jesus and his unique identity as Son of God come among us. Let me give three examples.

Deft Modifications

(1) Pullman's rendering of Jesus' visit to the home of Martha and Mary (Luke 10:38–42) begins by having Martha rebuke Mary for letting the bread burn: 'I ask you to be careful with it, and you just forget all about it.' In Luke's text, however, Martha complains rather to Jesus, while calling him by a title that suggests more than human status: 'Lord, do you not care that my sister has left me to get on with the work by myself? Tell her to come and give me a hand.' In what Luke reports, Jesus' reply implies something about his own personal significance: Mary 'has chosen what is best' by remaining with him and listening to his words.

Pullman's version plays down the importance of being in the presence of Jesus and hearing him. Jesus tells Mary to go and help her sister. Pullman moves our attention away from the unique person and presence of Jesus to stress the need for a fidelity to household chores that will not let the toast burn.

(2) When paraphrasing the parable of the Wise and Foolish Girls (Matthew 25:1–13), Pullman rewrites the story to highlight the action of one of the wise girls. She preferred to stay outside with her foolish 'sisters' and share the last of her oil with them rather than go inside to the wedding banquet. The kingdom of heaven, Pullman announces, was not inside in the bridegroom's house but outside in the darkness and with that generous wise girl and her 'sisters'.

By fantasising about the generosity of this wise girl and her solidarity with her 'sisters' in need, Pullman once again shifts the reader's attention away from Jesus. At the heart of the parable is the mysterious bridegroom, Jesus himself. Preparing to be with him takes precedence over everything else.

Old Testament prophets – in particular, Jeremiah and Hosea – had already represented God as the divine bridegroom in love with his people. When Jesus presented himself as 'the bridegroom' come among us (Mark 2:19–20), he laid claim to a divine title. Christians were to take up this image (2 Corinthians 11:2; Ephesians 5:22–33).

It would flower in the last book of the New Testament, which pictures the climax of all history as the 'marriage feast of the Lamb' (Revelation 19:9). The Lord Jesus will take the new Jerusalem as his bride (Revelation 21–22).

By the way Pullman rewrites the parable of the Wise and Foolish Girls, it serves merely to 'point a moral': forget yourself and be generous to those in serious need. He robs the story of its central, Jesus-related significance.

(3) Let me close with a third example of Pullman deliberately altering the main thrust of a Gospel passage, in this case the parable of the Prodigal Son, better called the parable of the Merciful Father (Luke 15:11–32). He takes it up in two chapters ('Joseph Greets his Son' and 'Jesus and the Family'). But he radically reshapes the greatest parable Jesus ever told and neutralises its religious impact.

When Pullman first retells the parable, it becomes the story of Joseph, now very old, welcoming Jesus home to a great feast after his thirty-day stint in the wilderness. Jesus had gone away without telling Joseph, who thought he might have been literally dead. The wilderness was full of dangers; anything could have happened there. Christ, the other twin, claimed to have stayed at home all that time. But this was a lie, since he had gone to play the role of the tempter at the end of Jesus' time in the wilderness. Christ resented the family feast that Joseph prepared for Jesus on his return, yet greeted his brother with apparent affection. All the same, a look that passed between the twins expressed their growing alienation.

Later on, Christ hears Jesus telling the story of a man with two sons, one quiet and good and the other wild and unruly. This time, Pullman paraphrases the parable more or less as we read it in Luke's Gospel. But the ending differs. When Christ hears the story, he knows that Jesus has seen him in the crowd and wants to mortify him exquisitely. Christ feels 'stripped naked' in front of all those people.

Here Pullman reshapes the parable in terms of conflict and increasing alienation between his fictional twins. He turns the parable into two episodes (one at home with Joseph and the other during the ministry of Jesus) that drive Jesus and Christ apart. This move effectively removes from the parable its central message or 'myth', if you like: *the unconditional mercy of God embodied in the person of Jesus.*

This rewriting of Jesus' greatest parable ranks among the most egregious examples of Pullman's tampering with the text. It might prompt some readers into asking themselves: should this book be renamed *The Good Man Jesus and the Scoundrel Pullman*?

Chapter Five

The Miracles of Jesus

Pullman recognised that he could not ignore what the Gospels report about the miraculous activity of Jesus. It is no viable option to pass over or remove that activity; it is too intertwined with the flow of the narrative in the four Gospels.

But Pullman cannot imagine the existence of an all-powerful, all-loving God who, for good reasons, suspends or overrides the ordinary laws of nature by curing instantly the diseased and disabled or by multiplying food and drink for those who need it. Pullman is not able (or willing?) to entertain the possibility of such genuine miracles that signal the divine kingdom being powerfully present in the person and work of Jesus.

Every now and then Pullman invokes 'magic' to account for the miraculous signs that characterised the ministry of Jesus. Thus he toys with the idea that magic might have been responsible for the alleged miracle at the marriage feast of Cana (p. 61). But how could a magician turn water into wine, which the guests then proceeded to drink? Or are we expected to imagine that all those guests were in fact drinking only water but they were bluffed into thinking that they were drinking excellent wine?

In general, reaching for such an 'explanation' slips over the fact that we do not find in the Gospels any stories of incantations, spells, conjuring tricks, and the usual stock in trade of magicians. It is with a simple word of command that Jesus works his miracles: 'take up your pallet and walk'; 'I do choose; be made clean'; 'young man, I say to you, arise'. Occasionally he uses 'sacramental' gestures, laying his hands on those to be cured, or putting his fingers into the ears of a deaf-mute and touching his tongue with spittle (Mark 7:31–37; see 8:22–26). But he refuses to have anything to do with the showy stunts of magicians and wonder-workers (Matthew 12:38).

Pullman normally rewrites the miracle stories by retrieving from nineteenth-century rationalists purely natural explanations. Delusion on the part of the observers, faith healing on the part of the 'cured' or some other 'natural' cause account for whatever happened. Thus Pullman entertains another suggestion about the marriage feast of Cana: the chief steward had hidden some wine that he hoped to sell later. But Jesus 'shamed him into honesty' and he produced more wine (p. 61). Here Pullman selects from the text of John 2:1–12 only what suits his rationalist purposes and shuts his eyes to what makes his 'explanation' quite implausible. John writes of six stone jars, containing twenty to thirty gallons each. Someone might have concealed behind a curtain a small skin full of wine. But how could the steward have successfully hidden six large jars containing 120 to 180 gallons of wine? As often happens when confronted with forced, rationalist 'explanations' of episodes in the Gospels, it seems easier to accept what the text says and, in this case, imagine that Jesus did change the water into wine.

A rationalist explanation also robs the episode at Cana of its rich, symbolic meaning. By providing miraculously a generous amount of excellent wine, Jesus offers a sign of the fullness of life in the new age of God that is dawning. The six stone jars, when filled with water, served for 'the Jewish rites of purification' (John 2:6). Jesus replaces the old rites of purification with the exuberant wine of God's final kingdom.

Five Further Cases

Let us see five further cases where Pullman explains away the miraculous deeds of Jesus. (1) We begin with the cure of Peter's mother-in-law when she was sick with a fever (Mark 1:30–31). 'Jesus went in to speak with her', we read in *The Good Man Jesus and the Scoundrel Christ*, 'and presently she felt well again and got up to serve them all food' (p. 52). Here, Pullman massages the text to imply a faith healing that took a little time ('presently'). Mark writes rather of an instantaneous cure in which Jesus did not say a word: 'he took her by the hand and helped her up'.

In an interview with Laura Barton (the *Guardian*, 19 April 2010), Pullman admitted that he could not read the Gospels in Greek: 'I have no Greek and it would take too long to have learned Greek for this purpose.' If he had known Greek, he might have noticed what was implied by the verb used of Peter's mother-in-law when she was cured: 'she began to serve (*diakonein*) them'. That verb will be used to describe the holy and courageous women who faithfully attended Jesus' death on the cross: 'they had followed him and *served* him when he was in Galilee' (Mark 15:41). When she was cured of fever, Peter's mother-in-law joined the ranks of those women who ministered to Jesus right through to his terrible death by crucifixion.

(2) Second, when Jesus exorcised a man and drove away a devil (Mark 1:23–28), Pullman has a 'natural' explanation both for the man's state and for his deliverance. The man 'was a harmless obsessive, one of those poor creatures who shout and scream for reasons even they don't understand, and hear voices and talk to people who aren't there.' Some calm words from Jesus let him 'wake up' and find himself again in the company of other people (pp. 52–53).

Before he is cured, the possessed man has shouted out in the synagogue: 'What do you want with us, Jesus of Nazareth? Have you come to destroy us? *I know who you are*: the Holy One of God' (italics mine). Pullman paraphrases the words and ends with the man asking: 'You call yourself the Holy One of God – is that who you are? Is it?' In Mark's text, the demon speaks in the name of other evil spirits ('us' twice) and states what he knows: 'you are the Holy One of God'. Unlike the human beings around Jesus, the invisible forces of evil already recognise clearly the true identity of Jesus and know what is at stake: a final battle between the kingdom of God and the kingdom of Satan. Pullman's paraphrase tames all this by inserting something not found in Mark's text ('you call yourself the Holy One of God') and by changing the evil spirit's statement into a question ('Is that who you are? Is it?').

(3) Third, Pullman turns a leper into someone whose 'skin was covered in boils and running sores'. He approached Jesus for help, because he wanted to avoid paying the cost of the lengthy and expensive ritual needed for his cleansing (Mark 1:40–45). When Jesus embraced him and kissed his face, the man felt better at once (pp. 62–63). Pullman drops Jesus' words of command ('Be cured') and reduces the miracle to a case of autosuggestion, prompted by a loving embrace.

(4) The fourth case concerns the healing of a paralysed man (Mark 2:1–12), which is 'explained' as another example of self-suggestion. The man felt so 'strengthened and inspired by the atmosphere Jesus had created that he found himself able to move' (p. 66). Pullman overlooks the way the story in Mark sets what is visible over against what

is invisible: the visible power exercised by Jesus in curing the disabled man as evidence of his invisible power to forgive sins ('my son, your sins are forgiven').

Pullman's way of handling the healing of this disabled man also turns up in more general terms. He assures us that 'some people who were sick felt themselves uplifted by his [Jesus'] presence and declared themselves cured' (p. 89).

(5) Fifthly, like many others before him, Pullman wants to account for the 5,000 being fed through the multiplication of five loaves and two fishes (Mark 6:34–44) as Jesus' good example prompting others to share the food they had brought. Someone had brought some raisins, another some barley cakes, another some fruit, another some dried fish, and so forth. There was plenty to go around when people generously shared what they had brought (pp. 89–90). But such a 'natural' explanation does violence to the text of the Gospel. Mark makes it clear that the disciples distributed to the crowd the bread and fish blessed by Jesus – not raisins, apples, barley cakes, dried fish and other food supplied by others. At the end, the disciples collected twelve basketfuls of scraps of bread and pieces of fish that were left over from the bread and fish blessed by

Jesus. They did not collect basketfuls of raisins, apples, barley cakes, dried fish and further food left over from what others had provided.

The examples given above illustrate three unsatisfactory features in the way Pullman retells the miracle stories in the Gospels. First, he feels free to change what he reads (for instance, in the case of Peter's mother-in-law). Second, his 'natural' explanations remain quite implausible (for instance, in the case of the excellent wine being miraculously provided at the marriage feast). Third, his reductive rationalism robs the miracle stories of their deep and enduring significance. Such cures as those of the leper and the paralysed man prompted St Augustine of Hippo to think of Jesus as 'the humble doctor' come to heal us both now and in the hereafter. The healing activity exercised by Jesus in his historical ministry prefigured what he continues to do, for example, through all the sacraments.

In particular, Pullman never notices a significance in the multiplication of the loaves and fish taken up by all four evangelists. Jesus' words of blessing, and his gestures in breaking the bread and fish and giving out the food, prefigure what he will do when instituting the Eucharist. There is a failure in imagination that cannot grasp how miraculously supplying ordinary food might prove a sign of the Bread of Life that, here and hereafter, feeds people spiritually.

Natural Explanations

All in all, Pullman doggedly seeks natural explanations that do away with the exercise of truly miraculous or divine powers. Thus he accounts for Jesus' escape from death at the hands of the enraged people of Nazareth by bringing some of Jesus' friends and followers into the story: 'They fought the townspeople – Jesus managed to get away unharmed' (pp. 55–56). Up to that point Pullman tells, more or less faithfully, what happened when Jesus returned to preach in the Nazareth synagogue on a Sabbath day (Luke 4:16–30). But then he slips in a group of 'friends and followers' who, like a friendly posse in a Western film, turn up in the nick of time and allow the hero to escape.

In Luke's story, no group of friends and followers intervene, and the episode ends with a sense of Jesus' own mysterious power. The people of Nazareth hustle Jesus to 'the brow of the hill on which their town was built, so that they might hurl him off the cliff. But he passed through the midst of them and went on his way.'

Chapter Six

Only One Source for the Gospels?

In retelling the story of Jesus, one of the strangest features that Pullman introduces is his attempt to derive all four Gospels from *one source*, Christ, the twin brother of Jesus. I have never before come across anyone proposing such an implausible notion and, in fact, making it central to his whole plot or thesis. Pullman's book is, of course, historical fiction. But *details invented in the cause of any historical fiction need to be convincing.* Current (and earlier) biblical scholarship reveals how Pullman's proposal of only one source lacks all historical plausibility.

The One Source

We are supposed to find it plausible that, encouraged by a sinister 'stranger', Jesus' twin, Christ, watched everything that his brother did, listened when he preached the kingdom of God, and kept an eye on the whole story: from the baptism by John, the temptation in the wilderness (where Christ himself played the role of Satan), the angry reaction to Jesus' words in the synagogue at Nazareth, through his acts of healing, the Sermon on the Mount, the multiplication of the loaves and fish, the hospitality offered by Mary and Martha, Jesus' entrance into Jerusalem, his conflicts with Pharisees and Sadducees, and right on to Jesus' arrest in the garden of Gethsemane (where Christ himself betrayed his brother with a kiss), the denial by Peter, the condemnation by Pontius Pilate, and, finally, Jesus' crucifixion and death on Calvary.

Sometimes Christ stayed cautiously in the background and received accurate reports from an anonymous informer who was one of Jesus' close disciples. Whether using this reliable 'spy' or personally witnessing it all for himself, Christ was constantly snooping around with his stylus and tablet to take notes of what Jesus said and did.

Later he transcribed his notes onto scrolls, often embellishing, distorting and simply falsifying the record in the interests of what he thought posterity could benefit from and accept. In Pullman's words, Christ 'made a better story' of what Jesus said and did, changed 'history', rewriting things as 'they should have been' or 'letting truth [read 'lies'] into history'. This falsified record would become the basis on which the institution of Christianity would be built. In doctoring the record, Christ was inspired by a sinister 'stranger' whose identity is never clearly revealed.

Here and there, Pullman drops hints about the diabolical character of the stranger, who at one point says, 'my name is legion'. This self-description echoes what the evil spirits possessing the Gerasene demoniac replied when questioned about their identity (Mark 5:9). In what he plans and does, Pullman's 'stranger' brings to mind Jesus' words about Satan: 'a liar and a murderer from the beginning' (John 8:44). The stranger treacherously deceives Christ into betraying his twin brother and bringing about his death on the cross. At times, Pullman calls the 'stranger' an angel, clearly a fallen angel. The chapter that seems to clinch his diabolical identity ('The Stranger Transfigured'), a parody of Jesus' own transfiguration, brings to mind Paul's words: 'Satan disguises himself as an angel of light' (2 Corinthians 11:14). This is precisely what Pullman's stranger does on a mountain.

Whatever we conclude, the stranger proves a demonic principle. He uses Christ to further his central project: a massive and thoroughgoing distortion of Jesus' teaching, along with a faked 'resurrection' from the dead that would bring about the foundation of the power-hungry Christian Church. It all leaves us with the question: is Pullman suggesting that Satan created the Church?

Multiple Sources for the Gospels

If Pullman had read such outstanding authors on the historical Jesus as Richard Bauckham, James Dunn, Martin Hengel, Craig Keener, John Meier, and N. T. Wright, he would have been alerted to the fact that, whatever their debates about details, all agree that *multiple sources* fed into the four Gospels. He would have learned the same if he had picked up any of the major current commentaries on the four Gospels: Ulrich Luz and John Nolland on Matthew; Adela Yarbro Collins, Joel

Marcus and Francis Moloney on Mark; Joseph Fitzmyer and John Nolland on Luke; and Andrew Lincoln on John. Standard introductions to the New Testament (e.g. by Raymond Brown) would also have shown Pullman how his picture of one source for all four Gospels to be found in the work of Jesus' twin, Christ, is, from an historical point of view, bizarre to the point of absurdity.

As regards Matthew and Luke, very many scholars endorse the 'two-source theory'. These two evangelists drew from Mark, the first Gospel to be written, as well as from a collection of Jesus' sayings, called 'Q' (*Quelle*, a German word for 'source'). Matthew and Luke also drew on other traditions: Matthew for such popular stories as the coming of the Magi, and Luke for some memorable parables (e.g. those of the Prodigal Son, the Good Samaritan and the Rich Man and Lazarus) and for other items (e.g. the cure of ten lepers and the story of Jesus visiting Martha and Mary). Hence it may be more accurate to speak of four major sources for Matthew and Luke – not only Mark and Q, but also Matthew's special sources (often called 'M') and Luke's special sources (often called 'L').

Testimony from eyewitnesses (in the plural) played its key part in the writing of the four

Gospels. Luke tells his readers that he drew on various eyewitnesses (1:2), who obviously included several women whom he names (8:1–3). In his *Jesus and the Eyewitnesses: The Gospel as Eyewitness Testimony* (2006), Bauckham has convincingly retrieved and defended two old traditions: Mark drew on a major eyewitness, Simon Peter, and John's Gospel came from another eyewitness, the beloved disciple. Bauckham also spells out the way in which the eyewitness testimony of the Twelve played a major role in the formation of all four Gospels. They lived on for some or even many years and exercised an effective control over the transmission of stories about what Jesus did and said. Not one (Pullman's fictional twin, Christ) but many eyewitnesses helped to create the Gospels.

Add too the testimony that came from numerous persons named by the Gospels: for instance, Jairus (whose daughter was brought back to life by Jesus), Bartimaeus (a blind beggar whose sight was restored by Jesus), Simon of Cyrene (who carried the cross for Jesus), Joseph of Arimathea (who gave Jesus an honourable burial), and Mary Magdalene, who along with other courageous women stood by the cross of Jesus and discovered his tomb to be open and empty on the third day.

Some, even many scholars, conclude that these men and women are named because they had provided eyewitness testimony for various episodes narrated by the four Gospels in which they had been personally involved.

Biblical scholarship, both today and in the past, has always agreed that the four Gospels come from a variety of sources. I have never heard of anyone before Pullman proposing that all four Gospels had only one source.

Why Only One Source?

In an interview with Laura Barton (the *Guardian*, 19 April 2010), Pullman told her that, before writing *The Good Man Jesus and the Scoundrel Christ*, he had read the four Gospels in three different translations. Even if he refrained from reading any scholars on the issue of sources, the introductions and footnotes that frequently appear in today's English versions of the Bible could have made him aware of the multiplicity of sources that fed into the four Gospels. Why then did he come up with the most improbable picture of the Gospels deriving from a single source, the scrolls produced by Jesus' twin brother, Christ?

This implausible thesis about the origins of the Gospels allows Pullman to represent Christ twisting and falsifying the stories by which Jesus would be remembered and on which a life-destroying Church would be founded. Pullman's antipathy to institutional Christianity shows through his 'one-source' theory.

This 'one-source' theory suggests a link between Pullman's book and Jeffrey Archer's *The Gospel According to Judas*, which retells the story of Jesus from the point of view of Judas Iscariot. Pullman does not literally do that. Yet he pictures Jesus' brother, Christ, eventually playing the part of Judas by leading a detachment of guards to Gethsemane and betraying Jesus with a kiss. Christ becomes Judas. If 'the scoundrel Christ' is responsible for all that enters the four Gospels, what we read in the New Testament is nothing other than 'the Gospel According to Judas'. In Pullman's fictional rendering of the origins of Christianity, the Christ who, under the malicious influence of 'the stranger', turns into Judas, is the one and only source of all four Gospels.

Before seeing how Pullman tackles the death and resurrection of Jesus, we should draw together the massive amount of rewriting in this story of Jesus. Pullman blames Christ and the smooth-tongued, malevolent 'stranger'. But are they not puppets in the hands of their brilliant and imaginative creator, Pullman himself? Who then is 'the scoundrel'?

Chapter Seven

Tampering with the Story

Pullman sometimes shines when his imagination fills out episodes like the cure, at the pool of Bethesda, of a disabled man whom he calls 'Old Hiram' (John 5:1–18). He pictures Christ, Jesus' twin brother, visiting the pool by night some days later and getting into a debate about goodness with a crippled beggar, a leper, and a blind man.

The lame beggar had been lying by the pool unwashed and unhealed for twelve years; 'the smell of faeces, urine, vomit, and years of accumulated filth rose from him'. Christ wanted to show some goodness by kissing him. But he turned away; the smell became too much. He tried again and kissed him very quickly. After he left the pool, he discovered that during their embrace the lame beggar had stolen his purse.

At times, the additions and changes left me puzzling about their place in the narrative. When telling the story of Jesus' arrest in Gethsemane, Pullman inserts a page about a crowd of curious onlookers, who had somehow heard about what was going to happen and turned up in the garden at two in the morning. They began to shout and jeer at Jesus, and would even have lynched him if the guards had allowed them to do so. Perhaps the narrative gains something from the hostile crowd being shifted from its place in the Gospels where they shout for Jesus' crucifixion in front of Pilate's praetorium (Mark 15:6–15). But the point of this change eludes me, just as it does in the case of the changes in the story of Zacharias (see Chapter 2 above).

Tampering and Omitting

Too often Pullman's agenda shows through when he either tampers with the Gospel narrative or else omits major features of the story that do not match his purposes. We have already seen numerous examples of his rewriting the Gospel texts: for instance, the story of Jesus' visit to Martha and Mary, the parable of the Wise and Foolish Girls, the parable of the Prodigal Son, and the event of the virginal conception of Jesus which is transmuted, apparently, into Mary being seduced by a young man claiming to be an angel. Let us see three further examples where Pullman tendentiously rewrites the Gospels: the baptism of Jesus, his 'Palm Sunday' entry into Jerusalem, and the institution of the Eucharist.

(1) Pullman's chapter on the baptism of Jesus offers yet another early example of his tampering with the Gospel stories. The Holy Spirit does not descend on Jesus. Instead, his brother Christ sees a dove flying above them and settling in a tree. Christ thinks it could possibly be an omen, and imagines what a voice from heaven might say if it were to explain the meaning of the episode. So much for the revelation of the Holy Trinity in the descent of the Spirit and the voice of the heavenly Father declaring: 'this is my beloved Son in whom I am well pleased'!

(2) As Mark tells the story of Jesus entering Jerusalem on 'Palm Sunday', a 'Messianic' demonstration takes place that fulfils a prophecy of Zechariah (Zechariah 9:9–10) about a 'peasant king' riding on a donkey and not in a war-chariot

(Mark 11:1–11). People spread their cloaks and leafy branches on the ground before Jesus, the anointed, 'messianic' king. As part of this victorious celebration, the crowd shouts a psalm of thanksgiving: 'Hosanna! Blessed is he who comes in the name of the Lord! Blessed is the coming kingdom of our father David! Hosanna in the highest heavens!' Jesus went into the Temple, taking possession with authority of the house of God. The following day he would return to take forcible action against the money changers and merchants who defiled the holiness of the Temple (Mark 11:15–19).

Pullman spends a chapter on Jesus cleansing the Temple ('Jesus and the Money-changers'), but he deprives the entry into Jerusalem of its messianic significance. Yes, Jesus rides on a donkey into the capital city, but people do not spread cloaks and branches on the ground nor do they acclaim the anointed king. Only 'one or two people had cut palm branches to wave', the rest bombarded Jesus with questions about what he intended to do (p. 150).

(3) In the Gospel narrative, what Jesus says and does when instituting the Eucharist during the Last Supper defines in advance the value of what will happen. His imminent death and resurrec-

tion will bring human beings communion at the final banquet in the coming kingdom of God (Mark 14:25). The words and gestures of Jesus at the Last Supper show him making a new covenant, ratified and sealed by the shedding of his blood. He wants to establish for countless others his continuing presence in the meal fellowship that he establishes with a small, core group of disciples.

But Pullman has nothing to say about the institution of the Eucharist or, for that matter, about what brought Jesus and his disciples together on that last evening, the celebration of the Jewish Passover. He merely tells readers that Jesus sat with his disciples and talked with them.

In a final chapter, set long after the death of Jesus, Pullman has the demonic 'stranger' dismiss the Eucharist as 'a little ritual' invented by none other than Christ, the brother of Jesus. It has proved a great success but the 'stranger' sneeringly asks: 'Who would have thought that inviting Jews to eat flesh and drink blood would be so popular?' Even though Christ had not intended the celebration of the Eucharist to be understood that way, the followers of Jesus, both Jews and Gentiles, have leapt to that 'lurid meaning'.

This way of reshaping the story allows Pullman to deride the Eucharist and its central place in Christian life. It is only a later addition. Worse than that, it has been misunderstood in a 'lurid' way that fails to correspond with what it originally meant when introduced by Jesus' twin brother after the faked 'resurrection' of Jesus.

Sometimes Pullman's rewriting of the Gospels may, however, be little more than incidental slip-ups. Thus he misreads the story found in John's Gospel about the piercing of the side of Jesus; he did not die 'from the thrust of a Roman spear' (p. 237). As the Gospel states, he was already dead when his side was pierced (John 19:33–34). Likewise, Pullman's picture of Thomas actually laying his finger in the still visible wounds of Jesus to settle his doubts (p. 237) simply follows a common misreading of what John's Gospel says. Jesus invites Thomas to touch his wounds. But Thomas does *not* do that; he at once blurts out his confession, 'My Lord and my God' (John 20:27–28).

Picking, Choosing and Changing

In his interview with Laura Barton (the *Guardian*, 19 April 2010), Pullman complains about the way people fail to give the Bible a full reading: 'they read the bits they like and ignore the bits they don't understand or don't like'. Has Pullman himself done just that? Has he read the bits he likes (e.g. the Beatitudes) and ignored the bits he does not understand or does not like (e.g. the Last Supper)? Has he also systematically changed many of the bits that he has read?

Pullman passes on the blame for such changes and falsifications to Jesus' brother, Christ. A complex character, he is cautious, traditionally pious, and his mother's darling. When 'improving' or simply falsifying the record he compiles of Jesus' ministry, he endows it with a miraculous glow and shapes it to fit conventional religious beliefs. No scoundrel by nature, he merits the label not only by systematically distorting his brother's career but also by two crucial developments when he plays the part of Judas and when, after the death of Jesus, he impersonates him as if he were risen from the dead.

'It is a fine study', writes Ronald Hutton (*Times Literary Supplement*, 14 April 2010), 'of how a good person can come to engage in treachery and deceit for the highest of motives.' Christ is led astray by the sinister 'stranger', who prompts him into engineering his brother's arrest in Gethsemane and tricks him into thinking that God will intervene at the last minute to save the life of Jesus. The 'stranger' knows that, if Jesus and his teachings are to be remembered through an institution to be organised, Jesus needs to be given a martyr's death and a 'resurrection' from the dead.

The scheming and unscrupulous 'stranger' represents the coming Church, or at least the leaders of organised religion as Pullman thinks of them. In the spirit of those who run George Orwell's 'Ministry of Truth', they will be ready to sacrifice history as it happened to 'truth' or what they imagined 'should have been'. These 'men of authority and wisdom', for whom the 'stranger' cynically speaks, will reshape the history of Jesus as they organise the Church and formulate the doctrines needed to hold it together. By 'magnifying Jesus', they will secure their own role as powerful leaders (pp. 145–146). This 'magnifying Jesus' refers to expressing the faith in Jesus that was to be enshrined in the creed that Christians recite on Sundays, the Nicene-Constantinopolitan Creed of 381 AD.

Such a picture of what went on in the first four centuries towards elaborating the common doctrine about Jesus being truly divine and fully human is nothing less than a nasty travesty. It is an ugly misrepresentation of what came from such leading figures as St Ignatius of Antioch (d. 107), St Justin Martyr (d. around 165), St Irenaeus (d. around 200), Tertullian (d. around 225), Origen (d. around 254), St Hilary of Poitiers (d. 367), St Athanasius of Alexandria (d. 373), and the Cappadocians, that wonderful group in the late fourth century who included St Basil of Caesarea, St Macrina the Younger, St Gregory Nazianzen and St Gregory of Nyssa.

Ignatius and Justin died as martyrs, and Irenaeus also probably died a martyr's death. During the persecution of Decius, Origen was imprisoned and subjected to prolonged torture from which he eventually died. A troubled figure, Tertullian enjoyed not power but authority for his brilliant writing and elaboration of theological terminology. In defending the truth about Jesus, Athanasius suffered much, not least through five separate periods of exile from his diocese, Alexandria. Hilary also suffered a period of prolonged exile for defending orthodox faith in Christ. Basil and his sister Macrina spent their patrimony founding and funding what was the first well-organised Christian hospital.

All of these people sacrificed themselves and some of them died as martyrs in the cause of confessing and putting into practice the genuine truth of who Jesus was/is and what he did/does for the salvation of human beings. Anyone who knows the story of such early Christian leaders would be astonished at the idea that they 'magnified Jesus' in order to achieve their power-hungry ambitions.

To be sure, there were some people who were ready to sacrifice history to 'truth' or what they imagined 'should have been'. But these were the Gnostics who were active from the late second century into the third century. They busily tampered with the good news about Jesus by adding alleged revelations and bolstering their own position as recipients of such 'true' wisdom. Pullman's sketch of 'men of authority and wisdom' fits the Gnostics and not mainstream Christian leaders, like Irenaeus, who fought against them.

Chapter Eight

The Agony in the Garden

In his review of *The Good Man Jesus and the Scoundrel Christ* (the *Guardian*, 3 April 2010), Archbishop Rowan Williams praises its 'limpid and economical' narrative but finds the flow of the narrative broken through 'a long soliloquy by Jesus in the Garden of Gethsemane on the night of his arrest'. 'Nothing in the narrative', the Archbishop observes, 'has prepared us' for what we read: as death looms up, Jesus declares God to be unfeeling and dead and abruptly abandons his faith.

What has happened is that in this, the longest chapter of the book, 'Jesus in the Garden at Gethsemane', we hear Pullman's own voice speaking. His passionate indictment of institutional Christianity will strike a chord in many readers and may attract or trouble them, according to their particular mindset or faith. It is with considerable eloquence that he expresses his own 'spirituality', or whatever one should call his plea for the loveliness of this world, 'every inch of it': from smelling 'frying fish on an evening by the lake' and feeling 'a cool breeze on a hot day' to kissing 'a pair of soft and willing lips' (p. 193).

In the Mind of Jesus

In the earlier chapters Jesus shows himself robustly confident about the love of God and the presence of the divine kingdom. He wants to liberate people from religious nonsense and hypocrisy. Unexpectedly in Gethsemane, Jesus 'admits to himself that there is no answer to be expected from heaven' (Williams). He has been proclaiming God as a loving Father, and now God is absent and silent. God seems like a grandfather who was loved once but now has died.

Beyond question, the passion narratives of the Gospels – and, in particular, Mark – present powerfully the terrible distress Jesus undergoes in Gethsemane and the loneliness he endures right through to his death on the cross. Yet he prays obediently in the garden: 'Father, not my will but thine be done'. On the cross he uses the opening words of Psalm 22 and cries out, 'My God, my God, why have you abandoned me?' In the terrible suffering he is undergoing he does not understand why God has failed to act and withheld his help. But what follows in the same psalm suggests a firm confidence that God will deliver him. His dreadful situation will be reversed. For Jesus, God remains truly 'my God'.

Pullman, I am sure, has never read any of those classical meditations on what went through the mind of Jesus in Gethsemane. Such writers as Peter Gallwey (d. 1906) in *The Watches of the Sacred Passion* credited the historical Jesus with enjoying in his human mind a knowledge about the whole future history of the human race. Hence they could picture Jesus as suffering intensely from knowing in advance hideous scandals in the life of the Church, the failure of many people to accept the redemption he was bringing about, and all the human sins to come. That foreknowledge, according to Gallwey and others, proved a major cause for Jesus' 'agony in the garden'.

There is a real resemblance between those classical meditations and what Pullman credits Jesus with thinking in Gethsemane as he foresees what will happen in the life of the Church: men of power punishing and even killing people in the name of God, putting 'heretics' to death to terrify the rest into obedience, taxing the poor to pay for their luxuries and great palaces, supporting crusades against nations they declare to be evil, and permitting the sexual abuse of little victims. Pullman pictures Jesus suffering from a chilling vision of evils to come and the knowledge that the Church set up in the name of God will often fail to be modest, poor, forgiving, and welcoming like a great tree that shelters everyone.

Pullman looks in vain for a Church that exercises no authority except that of love. In the soliloquy attributed to Jesus, Pullman ponders and develops effectively the image Jesus offered of the tree that will give shade and welcome to everyone (Matthew 13:31–32) (pp. 197–200).

Some Comments

This indictment of institutional Catholicism invites three comments. First, Pullman recognises earlier what Christians have done towards educating children, nursing the sick, and feeding the hungry. But these have been 'burdens for the faithful to carry' and *not* the work of their leaders (pp. 171–173). (This judgement, incidentally, does not stand up historically. If 'the faithful' often led the way in education, health care, and ministry to the needy, sooner or later they needed and received the support of the bishops for their work to continue and flourish.) After a nod toward the good deeds of ordinary Christians, Pullman repeatedly scarifies institutional Christianity and represents it as the 'work of Satan' rejected by Jesus in the wilderness (pp. 42–44). In the Gethsemane scene (see above), Pullman spells out various particular evils that this work of Satan was to commit down through the centuries. This case against the Catholic Church notoriously leaves us with the question: if the Church has indulged in so much destruction and self-destruction, why is it still there after two thousand years, the largest and most enduring institution known to world history? The fiercer Pullman's indictments become, the less he can account for the continuing existence of the Church.

Second, Gallwey and other spiritual writers of earlier generations never pictured Jesus suffering in Gethsemane through his vision of what ruthless and powerful atheists would do to millions of victims in their world. But what of Pullman himself? Unlike Gallwey and those spiritual authors, he writes after the end of the twentieth century, perhaps the most blood-stained century in all world history. Should he have woven into the soliloquy of Jesus some hint of the horrific evil that would be brought by such notorious atheists as Hitler, Mao Zedong, Pol Pot, and Stalin? Or does his dislike of organised religion so fill his imagination that it stops him from recognising the dreadful evils committed by godless regimes and rulers?

In the agonised soliloquy that Jesus delivers for ten pages in Gethsemane, his 'lips are moving but we seem to be hearing Pullman' (Thornton McCamish, the *Sunday Age*, 9 May 2010). No other chapter leaves behind so thoroughly the words of Jesus recorded in the Gospels. In it we hear what Pullman loves about the world and what he loathes in an institutional Christianity that seeks political power. But does he loathe anything in the history of the modern world? Surely there is much to indict there?

Third, Pullman is right in holding that the story of Jesus stands in judgment of what Christians

The Agony in the Garden

and their leaders often do and fail to do. Faced with the real Jesus, they can feel that he is 'asking too much' of them (p. 244). Thus the historical figure of Jesus comes into play to provide grounds for criticising, sometimes intensely, current Church life and failures in true discipleship. The experience of Catholics since the Second Vatican Council has shown that any efforts to renew the Church will remain spiritually empty, emotionally hollow, and doctrinally unsound, unless they draw inspiration and strength from the Founder of Christianity himself. But Jesus as a critic of Christianity is immeasurably more powerful and demanding than the merely human preacher of the coming Kingdom depicted by Pullman. A full picture of who Jesus was and is presents a person who has the right to ask from his followers nothing less than everything and to promise them also nothing less than everything. While Pullman rightly proposes Jesus the critic, he robs Jesus of his real authority by cutting him down to merely human size. If Jesus was only a noble and passionate preacher whose life and activity were cut short by those in power, what real authority does he now possess to reform the lives of those who profess to be his followers or turn others into his committed disciples?

Chapter Nine

The Death and 'Resurrection' of Jesus

In the passion stories of the Gospels, three men collaborate to bring about the death of Jesus: the disciple Judas, the Jewish high priest Caiaphas, and the Roman prefect Pontius Pilate.

The Arrest and Death of Jesus

Pullman's retelling of the Gospel stories respects the record of Pilate's ruthless brutality in dispatching Jesus to his death on the cross. He plays down the responsibility of Caiaphas and represents him as suggesting that Pilate send Jesus into exile. What Caiaphas says about the expediency of

Jesus' death (John 11:49) is maintained but conveniently put into the mouths of the 'stranger' and of Christ, the twin brother of Jesus who plays the part of Judas (p. 174).

Nevertheless, in the chapter 'Caiaphas', we do find the high priest putting the case for being 'constrained by circumstances' to arrest and proceed against Jesus. He is also in league with the demonic 'stranger', who seems his 'valued counsellor' (p. 187).

As we have seen, Christ plays the part of Judas in being paid to lead the guard to Jesus and identify him with a kiss. In Pullman's version, he does not, however, then give way to remorse, return the money to chief priests and hang himself (Matthew 27:3–10). Instead, in Pullman's rewriting of the story, Judas agrees to do worse by masquerading as his dead brother and deceiving people into thinking that Jesus has risen from the dead.

The 'stranger' has convinced Christ that the 'truth' (read 'lie') of the resurrection is necessary. This lie will bring great comfort to the sick, to starving orphans, and to dying women. The page where the 'stranger' puts the case for fabricating Jesus' resurrection is, in my view, the most cynical in the whole book (p. 174).

The 'Resurrection'

As in the Gospel narratives, Joseph of Arimathea, assisted by Nicodemus, sees to the honourable burial of Jesus. The 'stranger' organises several men to remove the body of Jesus during the night of Saturday/Sunday. He persuades Christ to return the next morning and play the part of the 'risen' Jesus.

Mary Magdalene, who has first discovered the tomb to be open and empty, then meets and talks with the twin brother of the dead Jesus. She thinks she has seen the risen Jesus and runs to announce the wonderful news to the other disciples.

Later the same day, the disciples, including Thomas, set off as a group for a village called Emmaus. Christ joins them on the road. They reach the village at night and invite him to join them for a meal. A disciple called Cleopas brings a lamp close to Christ's face and takes him to be the risen Jesus. Christ plays out the deception, encourages the disciples to identify him as his twin brother raised from the dead and, for good measure, leaves them with a 'sign' of his brother's 'resurrection' from the dead: bread that is to be broken and wine that is to be poured out.

An Unlikely Tale

Many of those who reviewed Pullman's book found little plausibility in the way he explains away the empty tomb and the Easter appearances. Right from New Testament times, sceptics have repeatedly accounted for the emptiness of Jesus' tomb by alleging that his body had been removed by friend or foe. Matthew 28:11–15 tells of guards being bribed to tell that the disciples of Jesus had removed his corpse from the tomb in which he had been buried by Joseph of Arimathea. The only new item added by Pullman comes when he attributes the removal of Jesus' body to a sinister 'stranger' who is intent on creating organised Christianity.

As regards the post-resurrection situation presented by Paul and the Gospels, Pullman ignores the appearance(s) of the risen Jesus in Galilee (Matthew 28, John 21 and implied by Mark 16:7), the appearance to Peter (1 Corinthians 15:5; Luke 24:34), the appearance to 'more than five hundred' disciples (1 Corinthians 15:7), and the appearance to Paul (1 Corinthians 9:1; 15:8; Galatians 1:12, 15–16; Acts 9; 22; 26). Pullman selects the appearance to Mary Magdalene (John 20:11–19) and the Emmaus story (Luke 24:13–

35), into which he slots the appearance to Thomas (John 20:24–29).

Some reviewers have spotted a hint of chauvinism in the way Pullman represents the credulity of Mary Magdalene. She meets the twin of Jesus and imagines she has seen Jesus himself risen from the dead. This way of explaining away Mary's experience at the tomb has a long history. It reaches back through the *Life of Jesus* by Ernest Renan (d. 1892) to the earliest known author to write against Christianity, Celsus in the second century. Renan built up Mary as *the* (hallucinated) witness, whose passionate love made her imagine that Jesus was personally risen from the dead and whose testimony convinced the other disciples. In his *True Discourse*, the earliest book we know to have been written against Christianity, Celsus dismissed Mary as a 'hysterical female', who, seemingly together with Peter, created belief in the resurrection of Jesus.

As regards the Emmaus story, Pullman feels free to play games with what he reads in Luke, where only two disciples walk to the village and then recognise the risen Jesus in 'the breaking of the bread'. Pullman rewrites, rather than re-tells, a vivid and beloved Easter story, for which the brilliance of Luke's writing has been matched by masterpieces coming from Caravaggio, Rembrandt and other great artists.

I can understand the reaction of A. N. Wilson (the *Spectator*, 3 April 2010) to Pullman's caricature of the Easter stories. Pullman not only remains silent about so much of the testimony to post-resurrection appearances but also leaves us with a strange puzzle. Could the early Christian witnesses have lived such heroic lives and spread the message of Jesus with such devotion if all that lay behind their missionary outreach were two episodes in which first a credulous woman (Mary Magdalene) and then a group (the disciples at Emmaus) mistook the identity of someone they met?

Pullman's version of what happened after the death of Jesus may be 'skilfully constructed' (Wilson). But is it so contrived and does it play so fast and loose with the evidence that it loses even its superficial plausibility? At the end does Pullman turn the greatest story ever told into the greatest puzzle ever imagined?

In an article (*Daily Telegraph*, 7 April 2010), Pullman let slip that for his reading on the resurrection he took up Geza Vermes, 'the great Jesus scholar', but no outstanding works on the subject by N. T. Wright and other contemporary experts.

Once again it should be remarked that, while Vermes did great work on the Dead Sea Scrolls, he would be called 'the great Jesus scholar' by very few, if any, contemporary experts writing on the Gospels, whether they be Anglican, Catholic, Jewish, or Protestant.

It is not that Pullman followed Vermes' reductive conclusion that other 'minimalisers' also propose: Jesus merely rose 'in the hearts' of his followers. My problem with Pullman is that he apparently limited his reading on the resurrection to a book that can hardly be called 'great'. The magisterial review of Vermes' study of the resurrection by Daniel Harrington (*America* magazine, 24 March 2008) pin-pointed its serious weaknesses and omissions. If Pullman had read true and recognised experts on the resurrection testimony in the Gospels, he might have had second thoughts about producing a banal, contrived 'explanation' of what happened to trigger faith in the resurrection of Jesus.

The Effect Not Proportionate to the Cause

If Pullman had read some of the classical (e.g. St Augustine of Hippo) and contemporary apologists (e.g. Hans Küng, Wolfhart Pannenberg and N. T. Wright) for the resurrection, he would have found the objection that Wilson raised being much more fully deployed. The 'reconstruction' proposed by Pullman, the body of Jesus being spirited away and then one individual (Mary Magdalene) and one group (some disciples at Emmaus) misidentifying his twin as if he were Jesus risen from the dead, is historically speaking quite implausible if we want to account for the rise and spread of Christianity. Once again, let me recognise that Pullman is writing historical fiction. But let me also once again insist that, by its nature, *historical* fiction should be plausible – also from an historical point of view.

History shows us an *effect*, the propagation of the Christian message and community throughout the world, a propagation that took place despite ruthless persecutions and other terrible setbacks. If Christ did not personally rise from the dead, what else might have *caused* this visible effect in human history, the development and massive presence of the Christian religion? Pullman asks us to believe that this effect was brought about by (1) fraud (namely, the theft of Jesus' body), and (2) a mistaken identification, deliberately prompted by a twin of Jesus masquerading as his dead brother 'brought back to life'.

That such an 'odd' turn of event after the burial of Jesus was sufficient to cause the rise and spread of Christianity will convince only the credulous, or rather those who simply cannot imagine that there is a God who raised Jesus from the dead and gave him a new and glorious life. They would rather entertain far-fetched 'explanations' than accept that the resurrection of Jesus himself truly happened.

The effect, the propagation of Christianity, remains a baffling enigma if one refuses to nominate the only adequate cause available, the resurrection of Jesus. The cause suggested by Pullman fails to match the effect. He leaves us with an enigma or, to echo Wilson, the greatest puzzle imaginable.

Epilogue

One huge plus about Pullman's book is that it promises to send people back to the New Testament where they will face the question Jesus put to his disciples: 'Who do you say that I am?' (Mark 8:29). I can only applaud that development.

The last few years have seen debates between militant atheists and believers being conducted on more general grounds. Has science buried religious faith? Has the discovery of evolution, in particular, made belief in God obsolete? Are faith in God and religious practice not only irrational but also socially and morally destructive? Or does belief in God enjoy rational support? Are there good reasons for thinking that a personal God exists and for living on the basis of that faith?

What has been happening seems a re-run of what happened in the eighteenth and nineteenth centuries, when believers allowed themselves to put Jesus aside and take up arguments about an abstract God-question posed by atheists and agnostics. By agreeing to bracket off the question of Jesus, it seems to me, they let themselves make a fatal move. Christian faith is thoroughly specific and focused on one person, Jesus of Nazareth. The primary questions concern Jesus himself.

Is Jesus the one who reveals God to us, that loving Trinity who are Father, Son, and Holy Spirit? Is Jesus the one who, together with his Holy Spirit, will bring sinful human beings back to where they belong and enable them to share the very life of God?

Hence, I feel very grateful to Pullman that he may encourage many people to face the central question posed by Jesus himself: 'Who do you say that I am?' In fact, Pullman has himself expressed the wish that his book 'might draw some readers to look at the Bible': let them see 'where I've changed something, or left something out, or put in something new, or transmitted it without alteration. I hope they'll read the Gospels for themselves'. In an interview with Jo Case (*Readings Monthly*, May 2010), he summed up this hope: 'Read the Bible! That's the "message", if there is one at all, of this book.' If we do read the Gospels and set them over against Pullman's book, what major questions arise and what conclusions might be drawn?

Four Questions for Pullman

The flap on the jacket of *The Good Man Jesus and the Scoundrel Christ* announces that this book 'asks the reader questions that will continue to resonate long after the final page is turned'. So what are my questions?

(1) One question emerges easily: did Pullman use or rather misuse the story of Jesus to wage war on Christianity? His distaste for institutional religion is well documented in *His Dark Materials*. What better way could there be for demolishing Christianity than by suggesting that it was founded on deliberate fraud: not on a true resurrection of Jesus, but on the theft of his body, and encounters with his twin masquerading as Jesus risen from the dead?

(2) Another question that resonates with me concerns the widely accepted demands of *historical fiction*. Did Pullman imagine that his picture of twins, Jesus and Christ, would enjoy any of that plausibility which historical fiction requires?

In an interview with Vit Wagner (*Toronto Star*, 10 April 2010) that was cited above (at the end of Chapter 2), Pullman explained how Jesus' twin brother was 'a fable, like the fable of the hare and the tortoise'. But fables, right from those of the sixth-century BC storyteller Aesop, belong with fantasy fiction, not with historical fiction. Fables do not mix historical figures into their story. You find the hare running a race with a tortoise but not with some famous Greek athlete of a previous generation.

Pullman blurs the difference between fable and historical fiction, by inventing the fable of a twin for the historical Jesus. He mixes this fable (which by definition is not based on history) with fact, the undoubted historical existence of Jesus.

The normally accepted requirements for historical fiction raise a further issue about Pullman's 'twins'. Did he really think that there could be any plausibility whatsoever in making Christ the one and only source from which all four Gospels drew to tell their story of Jesus?

In the *Observer* (4 April 2010), Bishop Richard Holloway praises Pullman's 'scholarship': 'there is no doubt in my mind that Pullman has a complete grasp of all the intricacies of the quest for the historical Jesus'. Has he? We saw in Chapter 6 above how imperfectly he has grasped something at the very heart of the quest for the historical Jesus: the sources of the Gospels.

The good bishop is deluding himself. Pullman himself has never claimed the scholarship that would enable him to grasp completely 'all the intricacies of the quest for the historical Jesus'. As we saw in Chapter One, he prepared to write *The Good Man Jesus and the Scoundrel Christ* by reading Pope Benedict, David Friedrich Strauss, Geza Vermes, and A. N. Wilson. He refrained from studying expert, contemporary 'commentators' on the Gospels; their findings and conclusions might have kept his fantasy in check.

(3) A further question may arise for some readers who are familiar with Jeffrey Archer's *The Gospel According to Judas*. The plot of that book involved Judas living on for decades after he betrayed Jesus; hence Archer had to cast doubt on references to Judas' suicide (Matthew 27:3–10; Acts 1:16–20). Did Pullman think that, while Archer rewrote only the story of Judas, he would

rewrite the whole story of Jesus and do so by using a Judas figure, a fictional twin who, influenced by a sinister 'stranger', falsified the record of Jesus' ministry, betrayed his brother to death, and then masqueraded as Jesus risen from the dead?

In his review in the *Financial Times* (12 April 2010), Cole Moreton points to what he calls 'a deep irony' here. Pullman 'has long accused the Church of prising open the gates in the story of the person who was Jesus and filling them with details of its own invention … But that is exactly what the atheist author is doing himself.' In Pullman's book, the smooth-tongued stranger who persuades Christ to spin the truth stands in for the historical distortions of the later Church. 'But as the author embroiders' the life of Jesus to 'reflect his conviction that there is no God, one could just as easily say that the spin doctor is Pullman himself.'

(4) Does Pullman have a message to sell? Could it be the message that faith is a delusion and institutional religion mere power play? As Christ says in the last chapter, 'this story' will be 'a tragedy'. The vision of Jesus 'could never come to pass, and the vision that will come to pass is not his'. Instead of being the greatest story ever told, the life and work of Jesus end in tragedy, a painful

tale of a wonderful idealist who was crushed by human power and whose memory was then manipulated by power-hungry Church leaders.

At the end, the sinister 'stranger' visited Christ and Martha, the woman he had married. When he left, Christ and Martha turned back to the table. They found that 'the bread was all gone and the wine-jar was empty'. The closing words of the book are utterly bleak and without hope.

In rewriting the story of Jesus, Pullman has nothing to offer his readers. The bread is all gone, and the wine-jar is empty. Once again: should his book have been entitled *The Good Man Jesus and the Scoundrel Pullman*?

A Failure of Imagination

Many people rightly describe Pullman as a great and imaginative storyteller. Perhaps the major failure of his latest book is a surprising one: a failure in imagination. He has taken a story full of puzzles, loose ends and apparent paradoxes, with a compelling, complex and elusive central character, and flattened out all the creases, making it neat, tidy, duller and, one must say, less surprising.

The pages of the Gospels fizz with a tension and ambivalence that have kept Christians guessing, arguing and troubled ever since. But Pullman's account solves the 'mysteries'. It displays a pretence of being rounded and complete. Everything is 'settled' in a way everything never is in a really great story – certainly not in the greatest story ever told.

The Good Man Jesus and the Scoundrel Christ: Interviews and Reviews

Brian Appleyard, interview, the *Sunday Times*, 28 March 2010.
Laura Barton, interview, the *Guardian*, 19 April 2010.
Craig Brown, review, the *Mail on Sunday*, 4 April 2010.
Jo Case, interview, *Readings Monthly* (Melbourne), May 2010.
Ron Charles, review, *Washington Post*, 5 May 2010.
Alison Flood, preview, the *Guardian*, 22 March 2010.
Julian Margaret Gibbs, review, the *Tablet*, 1 May 2010.
Charlotte Higgins, the *Guardian*, 29 March 2010.
Bishop Richard Holloway, review, the *Observer*, 4 April 2010.
Christopher Howse, review, the *Daily Telegraph*, 31 March 2010.
Christopher Howse, review, the *Tablet*, 17 April 2010.
Ronald Hutton, review, the *Times Literary Supplement*, 14 April 2010.
Stuart Kelly, review, *Scotland on Sunday*, 11 April 2010.
Thornton McCamish, review, the *Sunday Age* (Melbourne), 9 May 2010.

Diarmaid MacCulloch, review, *Literary Review*, April 2010.
Catherine Mallette, review, *Fort Worth Star-Telegram*, 21 April 2010.
Cole Moreton, review, the *Financial Times*, 12 April 2010.
Niamh O'Connor, review, *Irish Independent*, 18 April 2010.
Nick Rennison, review, the *Sunday Times*, 4 April 2010.
Tim Rutter, review, *Los Angeles Times*, 27 April 2020.
Rowan Somerville, review, the *Sunday Telegraph*, 11 April 2010.
Boyd Tonkin, review, the *Independent*, 2 April 2010.
Nicholas Tucker, review, the *Independent*, 18 April 2010.
William Underhill, review, *Newsweek*, 29 April 2010.
Salley Vickers, review, the *Daily Telegraph*, 2 April 2010.
Erica Wagner, interview, *The Times*, 3 April 2010.
Vit Wagner, interview, *Toronto Star*, 10 April 2010.
Archbishop Rowan Williams, review, the *Guardian*, 3 April 2010.
A[ndrew]. N. Wilson, review, the *Spectator*, 3 April 2010.
Jeanette Winterson, review, *The Times*, 14 April 2010.

Index of Names

Aesop, 96
Allison, D. C., 8
Appleyard, B., 24, 28, 101
Archer, J., ix, 62, 97
Athanasius, St, 73
Augustine of Hippo, St, 52, 89

Baigent, M., xii-xv
Barton, L., 6, 24, 48, 61, 70, 101
Basil the Great, St, 73
Bauckham, R., 8, 58, 60
Benedict XVI, Pope, 6–8, 97
Brown, C., 101
Brown, D., vii-viii, x
Brown, R. E., 59
Burgess, A., 4, 6

Caesar, Julius, 2
Caravaggio, 88
Case, J., 33, 95, 101
Celsus, 87

Decius, Emperor, 73
Dunn, J. D. G., 8, 58

Elizabeth I, Queen, 2

Fitzmyer, J. A., 59
Flood, A., 101
Fraser, G. M., 2–3, 6

Gallwey, P., 77, 79–80

Gibbs, J. M., 101
Graves, R., xii, xiii, xv
Gregory of Nazianzus, St, 73
Gregory of Nyssa, St, 73

Harrington, D. J., 89
Hays, R. B., 26
Hengel, M., 8, 58
Higgins, C., 101
Hilary of Poitiers, St, 73
Hitler, A., 80
Holloway, Bishop Richard, 97, 101
Hooker, M., 26
Hoskyns, Sir Edwyn, 3
Howse, C., ix, 101
Hurtado, L. W., 28
Hutton, R., 71, 101

Ignatius of Antioch, St, 73
Irenaeus, St, 73, 74

James, M. R., 17
Josephus, 18
Jung, C. J., 31–32
Justin Martyr, St, 73

Keener, C., 5, 8, 58
Kelly, S., 101
Kendall, D., xv
Küng, H., 90

Lawrence, D. H., xii, xiii, xv

Leigh, R., xii-xv
Lincoln, Abraham, xi
Lincoln, Andrew, 59
Lincoln, H., xii-xv
Luz, U., 58

McCamish, T., 80, 101
Macrina, St, 73
MacCulloch, D., viii-ix, 101
Mallette, C., 102
Mao Zedong, 80
Marcus, J., 58-59
Martyn, J. L., 26
Meier, J. P., 8, 58
Moloney, F. J., 59
Moreton, C., 98, 102

Nietzsche, F. W., ix
Nolland, J., 58-59

O'Connor, N., 102
Origen, 73
Orwell, G., 72

Pannenberg, W., 90
Philip II, King, 2
Podro, J., xiii
Pol Pot, 80

Rembrandt, 88
Renan, E., 87
Rennison, N., 102
Rice, A., 5-6
Rutter, T., 102

Sayers, D., 3-4, 6
Schonfield, H., vii-viii
Schweitzer, A., vii-viii
Somerville, R., 32, 102
Stalin, J., 80
Stegman, T. 26
Strauss, D. F., 6-8, 97

Temple, Archbishop William, 3
Tertullian, 73
Theissen, G., vii-viii, 4, 6
Thiering, B., xii, xiv-xv
Tolkien, J. R. R., 2
Tonkin, B., 102
Tucker, N., 102

Underhill, W., 102

Vermes, G., 6-7, 88-89, 97
Vickers, S., ix, 102

Wagner, E., 29, 30, 31, 102
Wagner, V., 21, 96, 102
Williams, Archbishop Rowan, ix, 34, 75-76, 102
Wilson, A. N., 6-8, 88-89, 97, 102
Winterson, J., 102
Wright, Bishop Tom, 8, 58, 88, 90

Yarbro Collins, A., 58

Zeffirelli, F., 4

green press
INITIATIVE

Paulist Press is committed to preserving ancient forests and natural resources. We elected to print this title on 30% post consumer recycled paper, processed chlorine free. As a result, for this printing, we have saved:

2 Trees (40' tall and 6-8" diameter)
1 Million BTUs of Total Energy
258 Pounds of Greenhouse Gases
1,166 Gallons of Wastewater
74 Pounds of Solid Waste

Paulist Press made this paper choice because our printer, Thomson-Shore, Inc., is a member of Green Press Initiative, a nonprofit program dedicated to supporting authors, publishers, and suppliers in their efforts to reduce their use of fiber obtained from endangered forests.

For more information, visit www.greenpressinitiative.org

Environmental impact estimates were made using the Environmental Defense Paper Calculator. For more information visit: www.papercalculator.org.